Kamala Harris
& The Future of America

CALEB T. MAUPIN

Kamala Harris
& The Future of America

An Essay in Three Parts

Center for Political Innovation
Dedicated to educating and fostering visions for a future beyond capitalism

Copyright © 2020 by Caleb Maupin

All rights reserved. No part of this publication may be reproduced, stored in a retrieval system, or transmitted, in any form or by any means, electronic, mechanical, photocopying, recording, or otherwise, without the prior written permission of Caleb Maupin.

Contents

Introductory Note

1. Where Did Kamala Harris Come From? 2
The Queen of Mass Incarceration - Not from the "Thin Blue Line" Milieu - A Child of the Berkeley New Left - Covert Manipulation of Leftist Politics - The Cultural Cold War - Two Factions in the US ruling class - The Trajectory of US Politics

2. Psychology Behind Politics 42
"That Little Girl Was Me" - Meet Donald Harris - "The adventurous and assertive one" - The Destructive Impulse - The Revolutionary Intelligentsia - The Emergence of Constructive Socialism - "Many Wonders and Signs" - Zbigniew Brzezinski & Susan Sontag - A Crude Freudian Manipulation

3. The Geopolitical Stage 85
A Fight Behind Closed Doors - The Honduran Coup of 2009 - Manipulating The Arab Spring - Conflict Within the Deep State - The Specter of Populism - The Snake - Education for Death - Single-Minded Son of the Working Class - Roosevelt and the Popular Front - A Crisis At Home and Abroad

Introductory Note:

This is not a biography of Kamala Harris, the Vice Presidential Nominee of the Democratic Party in the 2020 Presidential election. This is an essay about US society and global politics. This text is an examination of Harris' record and life story, and an explanation of the political, cultural, and psychological trends that created such a figure.

This text is highly critical of Kamala Harris, highlighting her negative attributes and digging into her life story. However, this text is not intended to make the case that she and Joe Biden are somehow worse than Donald Trump, or to compel the reader to vote or campaign in a certain way. The book has no loyalty to any campaign, political figure, or organization within US society at this time, and is not intended to compel specific political actions from those who read it.

This book draws heavily from Marxism and leftist thought, to examine one individual who is likely to be highly influential in the coming years, regardless of the November election results.

The text is divided into three chapters:
1) Where did Kamala Harris come from?
2) Psychology Behind Politics.
3) The Geopolitical Stage.

This book is written out of a deep love for the working people of the United States and all who have suffered from oppression. The reader is expected to come away with a deeper understanding of the current crisis in US society, its roots and the hope for potential resolutions.

It is written in the hopes of inspiring all of those who would dare to join arm in arm with the rest of the human race in the struggle for a better world.

1. Where Did Kamala Harris Come From?

The decision came late. August 1st had been the date when the Vice Presidential nominee of Joe Biden was to be announced, but the decision was not made until August 11th. Amid the confusion and anticipation, something was happening behind closed doors.

The US public got to know Kamala Harris through the months of delayed decision, as she appeared on almost every mainstream talk show, giggling, talking about her childhood, reflecting on her experiences with racism, and her hobbies such as cooking. *Politico* had hinted that Kamala Harris would be the nominee in what appeared to be a leak, but the Biden campaign made it clear that the decision had not yet been made. Kamala had seemed to be the obvious choice when Biden announced his pick would be a woman of color, but yet, new names suddenly appeared in the running, as if some desperate resistance to picking her was coming from various quarters within the Biden camp.

In the week prior to the delayed announcement, the media had suddenly begun highlighting former UN ambassador Susan Rice as an alternative to Harris. Suddenly, the relatively unknown Los Angeles Congresswoman Karen Bass was filling the headlines as well.

Almost as soon as Karen Bass' name hit the national media, she was subjected to an all out red-baiting campaign by the press. Mainstream newspapers like the *Washington Post* and the *New York Times* were pointing out that this potential Vice Presidential nominee had visited Cuba with the Venceremos Brigades during the 1970s and praised Fidel Castro. Much like months before with Bernie Sanders, these oddly worded press articles framed Bass as cozy with Washington's geopolitical opponents and thus unfit for office.

Information about Bass' travels and associations decades before that likely had appeared in some kind of intelligence background check or dossier, were suddenly found in the press. Bass was desperately reassuring the public that she was not a Communist and it became clear that Biden was unlikely to select her.

The schedule for the Democratic National Convention speakers, released just hours before the announcement of the VP pick, listed Kamala Harris as speaking in a separate time slot from the Vice Presidential pick. This was almost declaring she would not be selected. Harris was reported to have "unfollowed" Joe Biden on twitter just a few hours before the announcement was made as well.

When the news finally came that Kamala Harris had been selected, many were quite perplexed. She had seemed like the obvious pick months ago. Why the delays? Why the last minute scrambling? Why the incorrect Democratic National Convention schedule? Why had Karen Bass been raised from obscurity, only to be roundly condemned as a Communist sympathizer?

It is clear some negotiations had taken place. Last minute deals were made. Joe Biden's arm was twisted. A rival from the Democratic Primary race who had blasted him as being supportive of school segregation was now his running mate. Kamala Harris had even said on the campaign trail that she believed the allegations that Joe Biden was a sexual predator. Yet, all of this was water under the bridge.

Kamala Harris was Joe Biden's running mate, the Democratic Party's nominee for Vice President.

So, what was going on behind the scenes? Who was pushing for Kamala Harris? Who was desperately opposing her? Where does Kamala Harris come from and what does it teach us about American politics in our time? These are questions that will be answered by this short booklet.

Kamala Harris' career as a criminal prosecutor coincides with a massive increase in the prison population of California. Many aspects of her record are contradictory to her current image as anti-racist and opponent of mass incarceration.

The Queen of Mass Incarceration

Kamala did rather poorly in the Democratic Primary. Her personality and record doesn't really appeal to US voters, especially in the swing states Biden needs to win. The most damning moment for Kamala's 2020 Presidential campaign came on July 31, 2019. Rival candidate Tulsi Gabbard used her limited time during a debate to highlight Kamala's record as a criminal prosecutor.

Hawaii Congresswoman Gabbard crammed a lot into just a few sentences: "Kamala Harris says she's proud of her record. I'm concerned about this record of Senator Harris. She put over 1,500 people in jail for marijuana violations and laughed about it when she was asked if she ever smoked marijuana. She blocked evidence that would have freed an innocent man from death row. She kept people in prison beyond their sentences to use them as cheap labor for the state of California, and she fought to keep the cash bail system in place that impacts poor people in the worst kind of way."

Kamala had no rebuttal to these obviously true facts about her career as a prosecutor and Attorney General in California. In fact, Gabbard's statements were just the tip of the iceberg. Kamala Harris had imprisoned parents due to their children being truant from school, and laughed about it during a presentation.

Kamala Harris also mocked protesters against the prison industrial complex, speaking in a sarcastic voice, strutting around the stage of a Chicago Ideas forum saying "Build more schools, less jails! Build more schools, less jails! Put money into education, not prisons! There's a fundamental problem with that approach in my opinion... You still haven't addressed why I have three padlocks on my front door... There should be a broad consensus that there should be serious and severe and swift consequences to crime!"

The idea of "serious and severe and swift consequences" is something that seems to arouse Kamala Harris. She was desperate to have Kevin Cooper executed, and battled in court hoping to prevent the DNA evidence California Governor Gavin Newsom requested. The evidence was acquired against Kamala's wishes, and Kevin Cooper's execution was halted. She now says she "feels awful about this" and blames lower level attorneys for the decision. Kevin Cooper remains in prison though he has left death row.

Kamala's office as California Attorney General worked to prevent non-violent offenders from being released from California prisons, after the state supreme court ruled the prisons were unconstitutionally overcrowded. The reason to keep people locked was, "if forced to release these inmates early, prisons would lose an important labor pool."

Harris secured the conviction of over 1,900 for marijuana (a few hundred more than Tulsi's number), and did indeed laugh about it when asked if she ever recreationally utilized cannabis herself. Almost 2,000 people received criminal records and often jail time for doing something Kamala apparently did herself.

As she laughed about it on "The Breakfast Club" radio program, the video of the interview reveals a face that is clearly oblivious to the hypocrisy to which she is confessing. The lives she destroyed are a mere bureaucratic detail, forgotten and tucked away as she strives for more personal glory and fame.

When asked what music she had listened to as she smoked pot as a college student, she said, "it had to be Snoop," referring to rapper Snoop Dog. Many bloggers noted that the time in which Kamala Harris was a college student and the musical career of Snoop Dog do not align. Kamala's post-secondary education took place long before Snoop Dog's rap albums hit the shelves. She was most likely lying. Many Black voices have criticized the Jamaican-Indian American woman's various attempts to pander to the residents of the urban Black communities who she took delight in imprisoning as San Francisco Attorney General.

Writing for reason.com, C.J. Ciaramella writes: "Whenever Harris is pressed about specific instances where she was decidedly unprogressive, she dodges, misleads, or glosses over the facts." His research points out that as a prosecutor, Kamala Harris defended the Death Penalty, always running on a platform of keeping it in practice in California. She opposed increasing oversight of police officers and investigating fatal shootings. Her office fought against exonerating the wrongfully convicted, and protected the Orange County District Attorney's office after it was caught operating an unconstitutional jailhouse snitching program. Judges repeatedly called out Kamala Harris and her office for withholding evidence, not notifying defense attorneys of misconduct by drug lab technicians, and having a "level of indifference" when it came to unethical and illegal practices that could help secure criminal convictions.

Not From The "Thin Blue Line" Milieu

The behavior of Kamala Harris as the San Francisco District Attorney and as the California Attorney General is morally horrendous. The efforts to destroy the lives of innocent people and to manipulate the California legal system in order to do it should disturb anyone who believes in justice or who posses empathy, most especially someone with a leftist, anti-oppression world view.

How many non-violent citizens ended up behind bars or with criminal records simply for the victimless crime of smoking pot? How many innocent people were convicted due to her practice of withholding evidence to hurt the defense? What kind of person would actively oppose utilizing DNA evidence to exonerate people on death row? Did the potential of taking an innocent person's life not concern her? Clearly not.

Harris' behavior might make sense if she was part of the "Thin Blue Line" milieu. Police officers, their family members, the various police unions, and the Fraternal Order of Police often cultivate a strange victim mentality and reinterpretation of events. Adherents of this right-wing layer of US society believe "police brutality" is a liberal hoax, and that the annually occurring deaths of officers on the job are the fault of anti-racist activists. In the minds of those who operate within the alternative reality of the "Thin Blue Line", the US suffers from an overextension of civil liberties to protect criminals. They see the police as under siege from the radical left and an overly compassionate society that coddles criminals. This refers to not only law enforcement officials themselves, but also to various right-wing vigilantes and fanatics like the infamous George Zimmerman, who buy into this world view.

This viewpoint is simply contrary to the reality. The United States has more prisoners than any other country in the world, not just in numbers but in percentage. Juries across the country rarely acquit, and very few defendants even bother to risk going to trial.

However, the illusions of the "Thin Blue Line" narrative are often utilized by prosecutors and police officers to justify their own misconduct, the kind of misconduct Kamala Harris specialized in. Prosecutors and police officers who feel that racism is a liberal anti-cop myth often feel that they must lie, brutalize people, withhold evidence, and "fight dirty" in defense of law and order. Various TV programs and films feature a heroic "dirty cop" who breaks the law and flouts legal procedure in order to put away a "bad guy."

However, Kamala Harris is not the daughter of police officers. She does not come from the "Thin Blue Line" milieu. As shocking as it may sound, her parents were both left-wing activists. In Harris' autobiography *The Truths We Hold*, published in 2019, she wrote: "America has a deep and dark history of people using the power of the prosecutor as an instrument of injustice. I know this history well—of innocent men framed, of charges brought against people of color without sufficient evidence, of prosecutors hiding information that would exonerate defendants, of the disproportionate application of the law."

The opening chapters of *The Truths We Hold* describes how her parents met each other through attending civil rights and anti-Vietnam war protests in Berkeley, Califor-

The parents of Kamala Harris, Donald Harris and Shymala Gopalan were involved in left-wing activism in Berkeley, California at the time they married.

nia. She writes: "My parents often brought me in a stroller with them to civil rights marches. I have young memories of a sea of legs moving about, of energy and shouts and chants. Social justice was a central part of family discussions." Describing her parents, she wrote: "They went to peaceful protests that were attacked by the police with fire hoses. They marched against the Vietnam War and for voting rights and civil rights." She described being a toddler and attending a daycare that was "small but welcoming, with posters of Frederick Douglass, Sojourner Truth, and Harriet Tubman on the wall."

A Child of the Berkeley New Left

Indeed, Berkeley, California in the 1960s was the epicenter of a cultural movement that swept the United States and western Europe in what was called "the New Left." Both of her parents attended University of California Berkeley. In the year of Kamala's birth, students at University of California Berkeley had launched the "Free Speech Movement." The university administration had forbidden students from organizing around "off campus issues." The students demanded the right to engage in political activism on campus and engaged in a campaign of civil disobedience, eventually forcing the University to back down.

On October 1, 1964, a student named Jack Weinberg set up a literature table promoting civil rights. He was arrested but thousands of students surrounded the police car, blocking it from taking him in for booking. The students held the police car for 32 hours, setting up a microphone on top of it and using it as a miniature stage.

Later in December of that year, student leader Mario Savio had thundered his famous words to a gathering of student activists, saying: "There's a time when the operation of the machine becomes so odious — makes you so sick at heart — that you can't take part. You can't even passively take part. And you've got to put your bodies upon the gears and upon the wheels, upon the levers, upon all the apparatus, and you've got to make it stop. And you've got to indicate to the people who run it, to the people who own it, that unless you're free, the machine will be prevented from working at all."

In 1964, the year of Kamala Harris' birth, the New Left was in full swing, with the "Free Speech Movement" erupting on campus at the University of California, Berkeley.

The Communist Party, the Socialist Workers Party, the Progressive Labor Party, and various Marxist-Leninist groups were certainly involved in the Free Speech Movement and the various left-wing protests in Berkeley during the era. The Black Panther Party raised money for shotguns by selling Mao Zedong's "Little Red Book" on the campus.

Many of the most prominent leaders of the various remaining Marxist-Leninist sects in the United States began their activism in Berkeley. Bob Avakian, who now leads the Revolutionary Communist Party, was a Berkeley native and the son of local Judge Spurgeon Avakian. He was heavily involved in the Free Speech Movement and later the founding of the California Peace and Freedom Party. The Trotskyite International Socialist Organization was the largest Marxist cadre organization in the USA in the 1980s and 90s. The organization traces its roots back to the Berkeley Independent Socialist Club, Shachtmanite Trotskyists who joined the Free Speech protests. Jerry Rubin, leader of the "Yippies" who was a household name radical during the late 1960s, began his activism as an organizer of the Berkeley Vietnam Day Committee.

Events in Berkeley during the 1960s significantly impacted the entire country. Ronald Reagan's reputation among conservatives on the national stage greatly expanded as he pounded the podium against "the mess at Berkeley" and cracked down on leftist student activists as California's governor.

The Bay Area radical magazine *Ramparts* became an essential source of news and analysis for left-wing activists all throughout the country. *Ramparts* introduced the country to the writings of imprisoned Black radical Eldridge Cleaver, whose book *Soul on Ice* was widely studied. Cleaver eventually became a leader of the Black Panther Party after being released from prison.

The editor of *Ramparts* was David Horowitz, a young radical whose parents had been heavily involved in the Communist Party USA. Horowitz eventually became a neoconservative during the 1980s and repudiated his years of left-wing journalism and activism.

Covert Manipulation of Leftist Activism

As radical politics flourished in Berkeley during the 1960s, something else was happening beneath the surface. At the time it was only speculated about. Rumors of government drug distributions and covert CIA funding of Trotskyists persisted, especially among hardline communists, but nobody really knew what was going on for sure.

Now, due to leaks and congressional investigations and documents released by the Freedom of Information Act, we know that one of the most successful intelligence operations ever conducted by the CIA was in full swing. With the Congress for Cultural Freedom program, the CIA was covertly funding left-wing artists, writers, and activists in the hopes of re-directing them to oppose the Soviet Union and China.

The "New Left" was synthetically created as a makeshift intellectual barrier between the circles of free thinkers, intellectuals, and dissidents in western countries and the Soviet Union. The CIA's website currently brags about the program. New York City Trotskyite professor Sidney Hook, the lone socialist voice advocating a total ban of the Communist Party USA, wrote enthusiastically about the program asking for funds: "Give me a hundred million dollars and a thousand dedicated people, and I will guarantee to generate such a wave of democratic unrest among the masses--yes, even among the soldiers--of Stalin's own empire, that all his problems for a long period of time to come will be internal. I can find the people."

According to CIA.gov, the agency's work was conducted by "a cadre of energetic and well-connected staffers willing to experiment with unorthodox ideas and controversial individuals if that was what it took to challenge the Communists at their own game."

Ruth Fisher, a founding member of the German Communist Party who had joined the Trotskyists, cooperated with the program. James Burnham, another Trotskyist who eventually became a Neoconservative, threw himself into the covert operation. The official leader of the Congress for Cultural Freedom program was Irving Kristol, a member of Max Shachtman's Independent Socialist League who would later become the ideological father of the Neoconservative movement during the 1970s and 80s.

A number of cultural magazines were established in order to highlight the work of anti-communist leftists. In the United States the *Partisan Review* flooded the universities, highlighting the voices of figures like Susan Sontag, Irving Howe, Mary McCarthy, and Hannah Arendt. In Germany, Melvin Lasky set up *Der Monat* to highlight the writings of Herbert Marcuse, Theodor Adorno, and the Frankfurt School, a dissident group of academic Marxists who opposed the Soviet Union and critiqued consumer culture.

Max Shachtman was the leader of the "Third Camp" wing of Trotskyism that had rejected Trotsky's claim that the USSR was a "deformed workers state." He functioned as a kind of elderly mentor to a crew of young, CIA-backed "free thinkers" whose job was to manipulate leftists to oppose the Soviet Union. Shachtman eventually moved on to become the personal advisor to George Meany, President of the AFL-CIO.

Michael Harrington, a young intellectual mentored by Max Shachtman, authored a best selling book called *The Other America*, highlighting poverty across the United States. Harrington eventually worked in the Lyndon Johnson administration, overseeing the establishment of welfare programs.

With funding from the United Auto Workers union, Harrington established Students for a Democratic Society as an anti-communist, pro-civil rights campus activist group. Funding from the Ford Foundation, Rockefeller think tanks, and other powerful entities enabled the Institute for Policy Studies to be established as a "safe" outlet for left-wing criticism of US foreign policy and the military industrial complex.

To put it simply, The New Left was fake.

It was a covert strategy for opposing communism invented by the intelligence apparatus. Prior to the 1950s, the Communist Party USA stood almost alone on the vanguard of opposing racism. Black intellectuals like W.E.B. Dubois, Paul Robeson, Langston Hughes, and William L. Patterson joined the Communist Party and saw the Soviet Union as a key ally of Black people against racism.

In 1949, the Communist Party USA organized a highly successful conference at the Waldorf Astoria Hotel in New York City. Scientists like Albert Einstein, actors like Will Geer, composers like Aaron Copland, novelists like Howard Fast, and many of the most prominent cultural figures had attended and participated in a pro-Soviet peace conference.

The job of the CIA was to create a chorus of left-wing voices who could invoke Marxist language and the rebellious spirit found in many intellectuals, while covertly supporting US foreign policy goals. The stated aim was to create a way for peace activists and Black civil rights activists to no longer see themselves as natural allies of the Soviet Union.

The Cultural Cold War

In her memoir, Kamala Harris describes how much of her childhood was spent at an African-American Cultural Center in Berkeley called Rainbow Sign. This facility which functioned as theatre, musical performance space, and restaurant existed in Berkeley from 1971 to 1977, directed by community activist Mary Ann Pollar. It is unclear who funded the space.

"My mother, Maya, and I went to Rainbow Sign often." Kamala writes "everyone in the neighborhood knew us as 'Shymala and the girls.' We were a unit. A team. And when we'd show up we were always greeted with big smiles and warm hugs. Rainbow Sign had a communal orientation and an inclusive vibe."

Among those who performed there are a number of Black intellectuals whose work was covertly supported by the CIA as an alternative to pro-Communist and anti-imperialist Black activists. James Baldwin was a particular favorite of the CIA, and the covertly funded *Paris Review* magazine directed by Peter Matthiessen was used to make his anti-racist writings famous. The book *Finks: How The CIA Tricked The World's Best Writers* by Joel Whitney, describes in detail how the CIA covertly funded and promoted James Baldwin's work and sought to marginalize W.E.B. Dubois. Kamala Harris notes that Mary Ann Pollar was a personal friend of James Baldwin, and that he frequently visited the Rainbow Sign facility.

Rainbow Sign was part of what was called "The Black Arts Movement" of the 1950s and 60s, which was a continuation of the Harlem Renaissance. It highlighted the work of African-American poets, writers, musicians, and painters. Researcher Adrian J. Mack notes that CIA's Congress for Cultural Freedom program was heavily involved in promoting the work of anticommunist Black artists. The CIA helped organize the 1966 First Negro World Arts Festival in Senegal. Mack writes, "the United States controlled who attended the event and the government believed US representation would improve the nation's image during the Cold War era... It comes as no surprise that the United States had gatekeepers in place to support the logistics surrounding the international festival, since the United States was strategizing how to globally contain communism." (See "The Black Arts Movement, the Congress for Cultural Freedom, and Cultural Discourse" by Adrian J. Mack, Nov. 27, 2018.)

Kamala Harris recalls that she and her sister sang in a performance of *Free To Be You and Me*. The music from this 1972 feminist children's album, eventually produced as an ABC TV special in 1974, was certainly popular in liberal circles during the era. The songs and poems decried traditional gender roles, telling boys "It's Alright to Cry" and urging married couples to do housework together.

Gloria Steinem, editor of Ms. Magazine and the face of the 1970s feminist movement in the United States, was heavily involved in putting the album and TV special together. Gloria Steinem's ties to the CIA are well documented.

In 1962, the World Festival of Youth and Students took place in Vienna. It was a gathering of communist and anti-imperialist youth. The young Gloria Steinem coordinated CIA efforts to disrupt it. Steinem established an organization called The Independent Research Service as a front organization that attended the festival in order to do intelligence work. A *New York Times* article published on February 21, 1967 described Steinem's work at the 1962 gathering: "Gloria Steinem, a 30-year-old graduate of Smith College, said the C.I.A. has been a major source of funds for the foundation, the Independence Research Service, since its formation in 1958. Almost all of the young persons who received aid from the foundation did not know about the relationship with the intelligence agency, Miss Steinem said. Ironically, she said, many of the students who attended the festivals have been criticized as leftists. The festivals are supposed to be financed by contributions from national student unions, but are, in fact, largely supported by the Soviet Union. Miss Steinem said she had become convinced that American students should participate in the World Youth Festivals after she spent two years in India. "I came home in 1958 full of idealism and activism, to discover that very little was being done," she said. "Students were not taken seriously here before the civil rights movement, and private money receded at the mention of a Communist youth festival."

In her book *My Life On The Road*, Steinem described her relationship with the agency, writing that the CIA "In my experience was completely different from its image; it was liberal, nonviolent, and honorable."

Interestingly, *Free To Be You and Me* would eventually be continued by a TV special in 1988 that played a far more obvious role in anti-communism and geopolitics. In 1988, a follow up children's TV program entitled *Free To Be... A Family* that aimed to de-stigmatize single motherhood was aired as a joint broadcast of ABC and Soviet State Television. The program, aired in both Russian and English, featured *The Muppets* and attempted to build up trust for the United States among the Soviet population. Actress Marlo Thomas hosted the broadcast, which featured Bon Jovi, Robin Williams, Lily Tomlin, and Penn and Teller. The program was essentially an advertisement for the US media and Hollywood, reinforcing the position of the Gorbachev wing of the Soviet Communist Party, which viewed the United States as a friendly country that meant no harm to the Russian people.

While spy movies feature the CIA as engaging in James Bond like action adventures, one of the primary activities of the US intelligence apparatus is controlling and crafting US culture. Joel Whitney's book *Finks* describes how the CIA covertly worked within major Hollywood studios to ensure that feature films fit in with US foreign policy goals, for example.

Berkeley was very much the New Left's epicenter. Nearby in the Bay Area's Haight-Ashbury neighborhood, the CIA ran a series of experiments with LSD. What was later revealed to be known as "Operation Midnight Climax", a part of Project MK-Ultra, involved CIA agents distributing LSD all over the city. Prostitutes lured clients to CIA safe houses where they were held captive and given doses of LSD. People on beaches and in restaurants were randomly handed pills by strangers dressed like hippies. This program was discussed in depth during testimony before the Congressional Church Committee. The congressional committee investigated and exposed a wide range of illegal activities of the CIA and FBI during the late 1970s.

In an era when Marxist-Leninists were the primary geopolitical rivals of the United States, and global networks of Communist Parties existed to oppose US imperialism, manipulating left-wing artists was one of the prime activities of the CIA. The "New Left" was a cultural and political movement the CIA specifically engineered for geopolitical purposes.

While Marxist-Leninist parties focused on building discipline cadre organizations aiming to mobilize US workers to seize power, the "New Left" of dope smoking, middle class freaks was quite useful in pulling potential revolutionaries away from them.

It was in this intentionally cultivated and covertly supported milieu of non-communist radicals that Kamala Harris was raised. She does not conceal this fact at all, but boasts about it in the era of Black Lives Matter as almost a political credential.

Two Factions in the American Ruling Class

After Kamala Harris was selected as Joe Biden's pick for Vice President, conservative speaker Charlie Kirk tweeted "Kamala Harris is a Marxist." The fact that Kamala's parents had protested and her father taught economics from a Marxian perspective at Stanford University, is presented as proof in right-wing media that she is a full fledged communist. A similar atmosphere of anti-communist hysteria was created around Barack Obama and his family's ties to CIA-linked liberal activism and academia.

However, it is not only conservatives that make this error. Among leftists it is often assumed that only the right-wing are supported by US intelligence agencies. Liberals and moderate socialists may be decried as sellouts or compromisers, but it is assumed that their efforts could not be supported by the ruling class or the state apparatus. Among leftists, the general viewpoint is that "the movement" is a force for good and the entire state apparatus opposes it. This is an illusion.

Kamala Harris grew up in a milieu that did not support communism, but functioned as a barrier against it, cultivated following the failure of Mccarthyism. The political crisis of the 1960s and 70s can accurately be described as a division within the US ruling class.

The 1976 book *The Yankee and Cowboy War* by Carl Ogelsby describes a conflict among the rich and powerful in the United States that was underlying the turmoil of the era. Ogelsby draws from Carol Quigley and other academics to describe the "Eastern Establishment" of New England old money and big oil, which has a history of clashing with other sections of the rich and powerful, namely weapons manufacturers and industrialists.

In the 1960s, corporations tied to the defense industry, the FBI, and most of America's millionaires favored the Republican Party, social conservatism, and an increased role of the US military around the world. However, the Rockefellers, an ultra-rich oil banking dynasty, worked with the CIA to covertly fund abstract artists and leftist criticism of US society. The Rockefellers funded the research of Alfred Kinsey, who argued that sexual promiscuity and homosexuality were more common. They also funded the Birth Control League of Margaret Sanger, now known as Planned Parenthood.

The Rockefeller think-tanks such as the Asia Society and the Council on Foreign Relations tended to favor cooperation with western European allies and soft power rather than military escalation as a method for defeating communists. Despite being ultra-wealthy and vehemently in favor of capitalism, the Rockefellers were widely accused of being Communists by the John Birch Society and other anticommunist fanatics.

In his study of the political role of the American oil dynasty, *The Rockefeller Syndrome,* Ferdinand Lundberg wrote: "What is the fundamental cultural orientation of the Rockefellers? They are certainly "progressives," modernists, rationalists, children of the Enlightenment, anything but obscurantists (leaving aside economics and politics). But they are progressives strictly within the ambiance of a murky status quo, subject at most to slow and bit-by-bit change. They do believe in slow change because they know change to be inevitable but the emphasis is on slow. Whatever people find irksome about the status quo the Rockefellers believe is fully amendable to reform— eventually. Although mild progressive reforms, belief in treatment of symptoms not causes, they are far from being broad front political liberals."

In his book *Market Elections,* Vince Copeland wrote that in 1964, when Nelson Rockefeller denounced Republican Presidential Candidate Barry Goldwater, he was most likely responding to attacks leveled against his family by other conservatives. Defense contractors, McCarthyists, and others saw the Rockefellers as a threat. Copeland writes: "It was Rockefeller's own fear at the time- his actual fear of being inundated by right-wing opposition that was going for his own throat, regardless of his impeccable credentials as a bloodthirsty exploiter himself— it was this self-preserving fear that spoke about "fascism.""

Essentially, the question facing the US ruling class during the Cold War was, how can we defeat Communism?

The industrial capitalists and the military favored establishing an authoritarian and heavily militarized society that would reinforce religion and patriotism. Lots of weapons could be sold, domestic labor unions could be crushed, and society could be mobilized to lock down for an all-out effort to defeat the reds, much as Hitler and Mussolini had done in Europe prior to the Second World War. Henry Ford, J.P. Morgan, the National Association of Manufacturers, and General Motors had a history of sympathy toward fascists prior to the Second World War. They saw highly authoritarian and military methods as the best strategy for defeating communism.

However, the Rockefellers, the intelligence agencies, and the "Eastern Establishment" tied in with European capital, had an alternative view. They argued that the way to defeat the Communists was by stealing their thunder, enacting progressive social reforms, coopting social movements, and thus stabilizing US society. The "Cold War Liberals" presented a kind of "anti-totalitarianism" similar to the perspective presented on TV programs like *The Twilight Zone*. The enemy is "Totalitarianism" of which Communism and Fascism are merely alternative brands. Liberal ideals like freedom of speech, freedom of religion, and equal rights should be maximized, the authoritarian tendencies of the military should be restricted, all in order to disprove the allegations of Marxist agitators and prevent greater social unrest and tensions.

The Trajectory of US Politics

The rise of Kamala Harris to the position of Democratic Vice Presidential Nominee in 2020 fits in with the trajectory of political and cultural battles that have taken place in the United States since the end of the Second World War. In the post-WW2 era, different interests and groupings within the US capitalist class have been directing the state apparatus in an effort to control the domestic population and beat back the rise of anti-imperialist and socialist governments around the world.

Political discourse in the United States has evolved based on the needs of different factions within the ruling class domestically and internationally. Reviewing quickly how US politics and culture has evolved since the end of the Second World War will ultimately explain where Kamala Harris came from.

A. McCarthyism (1946-1956)

From 1946 to 1956, US politics was dominated by a right-wing mobilization referred to as McCarthyism. The US ruling class saw the expansion of the socialist camp in Eastern Europe and the rising popularity of Communism around the world, and mobilized to weaken any Marxist influence at home. The newly widespread accessibility of television enabled the population to be very effectively psyched up into fear of the Soviet Union and hatred toward Communists.

In the first years of McCarthyism, the Roosevelt wing of the Democratic Party, which favored cooperation with the Soviet Union and had deep roots in organized labor, was crushed. Figures like Henry Wallace and Alger Hiss were demonized as Soviet agents. The Communist Party USA's national leadership was imprisoned, and Communists were barred from the leadership of labor unions. Hollywood screenwriters and actors were called before Congressional committees and jailed for refusing to name names.

In 1949, the victory of the Chinese Revolution emboldened the anti-Communist hysteria. Republicans declared that the Democratic Party had "lost China" to the Reds. Republican Senator Joe McCarthy ascended to popularity, decrying an alleged Communist conspiracy within the US State Department. A crackdown, not just on left-wing activism, but also on homosexuality and pornography, took place across the country. The 1951 McCarran Internal Security Act assigned the US Justice Department to assemble a list of 2 million people to be placed in concentration camps amid a national emergency.

In 1953, Julius and Ethel Rosenberg were executed despite widespread opposition both domestically and internationally. After Stalin's death, it became clear that his successors favored negotiating with the United States and were willing to restrain Soviet aligned activists around the world in exchange for a softening of relations. However, much of the US population was still reeling with anti-communism and was hostile to such negotiations. Many middle class elements utilized McCarthyism to express their rage at the ultra-rich and powerful institutions in US society.

In 1954, Joe McCarthy accused the US Army of being controlled by Communists. The extreme right opposed the strategy of utilizing Tito's Yugoslavia as an ally against the Soviet Union in Eastern Europe. Institutions like the Methodist Church became the target of McCarthyist allegations. US Senator Lester C. Hunt committed suicide in response to McCarthy's threats against him.

US mainstream media turned against Joe McCarthy largely because many believed his activities were hurting US foreign policy and causing domestic instability. McCarthy was censured by the US Congress and eventually drank himself to death. The Hollywood blacklists gradually faded and the atmosphere of hysterical anticommunism died down as the decade went on.

B. The New Left (1961-1972)

In response to McCarthyism, a wave of liberal anti-totalitarianism expanded. The northern wing of the Democratic Party, including the Kennedy family, embraced the

Civil Rights Movement. Much of the activism of Martin Luther King, Jr. was directly paid for by the United Auto Workers Union. Many liberal elements felt that Jim Crow Segregation made the United States look hypocritical in its denunciations of the Soviet Union, and that the race question was a ticking time bomb which Communists could utilize to sew unrest.

In 1961, Republican President Dwight Eisenhower warned about the dangerous influence of weapons manufacturers and war profiteers in Washington DC. On national television he stated "In the councils of government, we must guard against the acquisition of unwarranted influence, whether sought or unsought, by the military–industrial complex. The potential for the disastrous rise of misplaced power exists, and will persist." Many within the intelligence apparatus felt covert methods were more effective in defeating Communists, but that the influence of weapons manufacturers on elected officials made big wars with mass bombings of civilians hard to prevent.

As early as the 1950s, the CIA had begun covertly funding "The New Left" as a way to prevent the millions of young liberals reacting negatively to McCarthyism and militarism from becoming Communists. The Congress for Cultural Freedom program spawned a layer of anti-totalitarian, "free-thinkers" who pushed a message opposing conformity and equating Soviet Communism with Nazi Fascism. Among this crowd of liberal artists and academics is where Kamala Harris' parents met at UC Berkeley. Her memoirs confirm that she spent her childhood among it, attending civil rights marches and singing in performances at Rainbow Sign Cultural Center.

Articulating the sentiments of Cold War liberals, John F. Kennedy said "Those who make peaceful revolution impossible, make violent revolution inevitable" and argued that the best way to prevent Communist revolutions was by industrializing and stabilizing third world countries with foreign aid. Following Kennedy's assassination, the Vietnam War escalated. CIA linked intellectuals like Zbigniew Brzezinski formed the National Committee for a Political Settlement in Vietnam, also known as "Negotiate Now!" France and other European countries became vocally critical of US military involvement in Vietnam. As the CIA pushed for a de-escalation of the Vietnam War, American media oversaw a cultural revolution. Talk of the "generation gap" was widespread, as the younger generation became enthusiastic about Rock and Roll music and hippie counter-culture. Drug use became widespread.

US Attorney General Ramsey Clark presented a sympathetic face to the Civil Rights Movement and dispatched Federal Agents to enforce the Civil Rights Act and Voting Rights Act. Clark attempted to restrain the FBI's efforts against the civil rights and peace movements. Clark also released a number of federal prisoners.

However, the efforts of the Cold War liberals did not result in a de-escalation domestically or internationally. In 1968, the underlying political unrest among African-Americans and white college students exploded into massive social unrest. The year began with the Tet Offensive in Vietnam, a huge, unpredicted wave of defeats for US forces at the hands of the Communist-led National Liberation Front.

After the assassination of Dr. Martin Luther King, Jr. in April, urban rebellions swept the country, and the national guard was dispatched across the country. At the Democratic National Convention in Chicago, peace activists clashed with the police in response to the nomination of pro-Vietnam war candidate Hubert Humphrey against the wishes of the majority of rank and file democrats.

Students for a Democratic Society, originally formed as an anti-communist liberal activist group, became dominated by Marxist-Leninist factions, and eventually split at its 1969 convention. Within the New Left, Communist factions had maneuvered effectively and gained influence over many young activists. Protests across the country became more militant and often featured Vietnamese flags. The Black Panther Party, a Marxist-Leninist organization of armed African Americans, became wildly popular. The group had ties to China, the Soviet Union, North Korea, Libya, and many other anti-imperialist states.

The feeling among the US elite was that just as McCarthyism had gotten out of control, now the New Left had gotten also out of control. Society at home was unstable and the rabble were making their international efforts difficult, once again.

While the Rockefellers had long distrusted him, Richard Nixon was victorious in the 1968 election promising to end the wave of social unrest. Richard Nixon ran as the "law and order candidate" who represented the "silent majority" that was disgusted with protests and urban rebellions. Nixon fired Ramsey Clark, and allowed the FBI to crush the Black Panther Party.

Nixon escalated and then ended the Vietnam War, and enacted a series of dramatic reforms to US society in the hopes of quelling unrest. Nixon lowered the voting age to 18, created the Environmental Protection Agency, enacted federal affirmative action policies in hiring, and followed the foreign policy strategy of Henry Kissinger, meeting with Mao and utilizing China as an ally against the Soviet Union.

Despite effectively ending the political crisis of 1968-1972 with a combination of heavy political repression and social reforms, Nixon was forced out of office following the Watergate Scandal. The press viewed him as a right-wing fanatic with authoritarian tendencies.

C. Neoconservativism & The Religious Right (1974-2004)

Following the political turmoil created by the New Left and the clash within the US ruling class over civil rights and the Vietnam war, what can be called the "Late Cold War Normal" in US politics gradually began to set in.

Nixon had utilized a kind of psuedo-populist contempt for Black activists and student radicals in order to win the elections. Hit songs like Merle Haggard's "Okie from Muskogee" voiced the opposition to the New Left and held the attention of many white working class people across the country. In 1970, Nixon supporters among New York City's construction workers launched "Hard Hat Riots" and began beating up anti-war protesters. Bumper stickers with slogans like "My Country, Right or Wrong" popularized the idea that dissidents and protesters were disloyal to the country.

This all fit the political strategy of Leo Strauss, a philosophy professor who mentored many students who went on to become prominent intellectuals and political figures in the United States. He argued that politics should be dumbed down and that average Americans should see it in simplistic terms. An article from *The Nation* described Strauss' influence as "Intellectuals, he believed, would have to spread an ideology of good and evil, whether they believed it or not, so that the American people could be mobilized against the enemies of freedom. For this reason

Strauss, we learn in one of many telling asides, was a huge fan of the TV series *Gunsmoke* and its Manichean depiction of good and evil." ("Beware the Holy War" by Peter Bergen, June 2, 2005.)

A trend among US elites favored military interventionism while dumbing down political discourse and portraying the left as disloyal and deranged intellectuals. This became known as "Neoconservatism." The academic field nicknamed "Sovietology" that focused on Cold War strategy became dominated by this kind of thinking. Irving Kristol, once the director of the CIA's Congress for Cultural Freedom, became a primary theorist of the Neoconservative movement along with Leo Strauss.

The Republican Party began making overtures to a particular faction among the hippie counterculture known as "Jesus People" or "Jesus Freaks." Religion, an important plank of American conservatism, was in crisis as young people became increasingly irreverent and cynical during the political crisis of 1968-1972. Despite the irreverence of their peers and fellow counter-culture enthusiasts, the "Jesus People" stood on street corners singing hymns and preaching Christianity while opposing the Vietnam War and supporting Civil Rights.

The right saw an opening, and a fanatical anti-communist pastor from South Korea, Reverend Sun Myung Moon, was imported to the United States. Moon had long been cooperating with US intelligence, and in the United States he began recruiting young people to his "peace movement" that supported Richard Nixon. Moon's followers appeared to be part of the counterculture, but their beliefs aligned with weapons manufacturers and the Republican Party. Moon owned a number of weapons manufacturing facilities himself, having acquired the copyright to producing M16 rifles in South Korea. Moon's followers became foot soldiers of the neoconservatives, setting the stage for what would eventually become a much bigger trend. Tony Alamo, a Beatles marketer who worked in the music industry, launched his own cult among "The Jesus People." His followers recruited teenage runaways in Los Angeles and much like Moon, despite the hippie aesthetics, they aligned with Republicans and weapons manufacturers.

Nixon's spiritual advisor, the famed evangelist Reverend Billy Graham, began featuring long haired, guitar playing youth on his televised broadcasts. "The Jesus People" suddenly became far more widely promoted in American media, though their politics were dramatically shifting. In 1974, Baptist minister Rev. Jerry Falwell launched an organization called "The Moral Majority" that pushed conservative politics enmeshed in religious fanaticism. All of this eventually culminated in a process of conservative protestant Christianity in the United States reinventing itself.

By the late 1970s, what would be described as the "religious right" of the Republican Party, patriotic, anti-communist, and military aligned conservatives emerged to re-energize the right-wing. They were aligned with weapons manufacturers, they were fanatically anticommunist, and they were ardent supporters of Israel. The "hard hats" of patriotic working class conservatives who favored the military, along with religious fanatics singing rock and roll hymns and promoting a dumbed down version of Christianity, formed the core of solid support that held US society together for the remainder of the Cold War and up into the 21st century.

The Reagan White House solidified Neoconservatism as a political trend. The Republicans favored a military escalation against Communists while opposing homosexuality and abortion. In the new "Late Cold War Normal" Republicans wrapped themselves in patriotism, anti-communism, and Christianity, as did the democrats, though to a somewhat milder degree. Divisions in the ruling class seemed to be pretty much smoothed over during the 1980s. Reagan was known for saying, "We are all friends after six", indicating that differences among Democrats and Republicans were not significant.

The Neoconservatives and the religious right functioned as the "hardliners" of America, who dominated key state institutions. Liberals who essentially agreed with their narrative of world events just favored a softer approach. Bill Clinton's Democratic Leadership Council pushed the Democratic Party further to the right, putting it more in line with the overall neocon agenda.

Mass incarceration was a big part of the "Late Cold War Normal." The "war on drugs" dramatically increased the prison population, with Democrats and Republicans both emphasizing a tone of "tough on crime" in their rhetoric. The "lock 'em up" rhetoric and policies that Kamala Harris is closely associated with had emerged in the 1980s but continued to expand in the following decade. Kamala Harris began working as a deputy district attorney in Alameda County, California in 1990. Eventually she became assistant district attorney for San Francisco in 1998.

Kamala's formative years were working within the prosecutorial side of the criminal justice system in California, as the state's prison population exploded. According to the *San Francisco Gate*: "The number of people incarcerated in federal and state prisons and county jails in California grew by nearly 40 percent between 1990 and 2000 to a total of 249,000 inmates. Although the jump outstripped the state's population increase of 14 percent, it represented a major slowdown since the 1980s, when the state's prison and jail populations exploded by an unprecedented 228 percent." (SF Gate, August 9, 2001.)

These were the years when talk of "superpredators," a pseudo-psychological term used to demonize young African American men, was all over television. The media routinely demonized Black culture, blaming rap music for crime, and stoking up a fear of gangs used to justify police crackdowns. Across the country, testimony from "Gang Experts" with no direct knowledge about cases helped convict defendants in court. The gang experts would tell horrifying stories that terrified jurors about how potentially dangerous an accused Black male was, securing the convictions of many African American men.

The Los Angeles Rebellion of 1992 in response to the Rodney King Verdict, and the 1995 Black Nationalist rally in Washington DC called The Million Man March led by Minister Louis Farrakhan, represented a significant push back against the rising police state from the African American community. However, few within either the Democratic or Republican parties were sympathetic to these uprisings. Huge protests and an unexpected wave of international opposition prevented the execution of former Black Panther leader Mumia Abu Jamal in 1996.

The "Late Cold War Normal" of US politics persisted long after the fall of the Soviet Union. This set up of "hardliner" neocons and evangelicals as the solid core of US society with liberals as their loyal opposition persisted into the final years of the Bush administration, when the financial crisis and the new realities of the geopolitical stage forced an adjustment.

D. Obama, New Atheists, & Privilege Politics

In response to the Sept. 11th attacks, the United States led NATO countries to invade Afghanistan, and shortly afterward the USA unilaterally invaded Iraq. The neoconservative core at the center of the US state apparatus was emboldened. These moves came at heavy cost to the United States in terms of long term geopolitical strength.

Demonization of Islam became central in the rhetoric of neoconservatives, Israel supporters, and evangelical Christians. George W. Bush even used the term "crusade" in reference to his war on terror, sparking outrage across the Muslim world. In the middle east, the USA has long depended on covert support from the Muslim Brotherhood, Wahabbi fanatics, and others who took deep offense to these sentiments and became distrustful of the United States. Furthermore, many NATO countries had opposed the US invasion of Iraq, and tension between the USA and the countries of the European Union escalated.

Meanwhile, the result of Bush's invasion of Iraq, as well as sanctions imposed on Iran and other factors, was a huge surge in oil prices. Not only did the high prices generate huge revenue for US oil companies, but the various anti-imperialist states that sell oil on the international markets significantly gained financially.

Russia's economy, restructured by Putin beginning in 1999 to be centered around Gazprom and Rosneft, state-run energy firms, surged ahead as oil prices increased state revenue. The Islamic Republic of Iran's "hardliner" faction regained strength in response to increased US hostility and significantly higher oil revenue, with vehement anti-imperialist and anti-capitalist Ahmadinejad being elected. Iran-backed Hezbollah became highly admired by the Muslims of the world for handing a humiliating defeat to Israel in 2006.

In Venezuela, Hugo Chavez utilized the high oil revenue to fund his projects for moving the country toward 21st Century Socialism. Inspired by his success and aligned with Cuba, Bolivarian Socialist governments emerged in Bolivia, Nicaragua, and Ecuador.

Meanwhile, episodes of racial unrest broke out sporadically out across the United States in response to instances of police brutality. Technology made it easier to record the actions of police with mobile phones. The lack of an adequate response to Hurricane Katrina in 2005 sparked huge amounts of anger from the African-American community.

Wages and living standards among average Americans had been significantly decreasing since the late 1970s. Home foreclosures began to increase among African-American neighborhoods in Michigan, Ohio, and California, but soon spread to communities across the nation, culminating in the financial crisis of 2008-2009 when "the housing bubble burst."

Amid financial collapse and rising geopolitical opposition, Barack Obama strolled into the presidency giving Messianic speeches with a wave of fanatical young supporters. His rise came as a result of two significant ideological blows being dealt to the neocon core that sat at the center of the "Late Cold War Normal."

The first blow came against the religious right in the form of a widespread and well promoted trend of religious skepticism. The internet and promotion from liberal newspapers like the *New York Times* enabled figures like Richard Dawkins, Sam Harris, Christopher Hitchens, and others to garner huge amounts of attention as they presented the age-old arguments of religious skeptics.

The beliefs of the religious right, namely that the Bible is the literal and infallible word of God, became subject to widespread mockery. TV programs, internet publications, and many prominent voices in US society began to dissect the kind of thinking which Jerry Falwell and Billy Graham had pioneered in the 1970s. The influence of the religious right, an important faction with influence in the US military, significantly decreased, especially among younger Americans.

Meanwhile, talk of "white privilege," a concept originally developed by Marxist academics like Noel Ignatiev, became widespread in universities. The idea that racism was a "thing of the past" was suddenly replaced with an understanding that African-Americans face many hardships in life due to their skin color, and that denying this was in itself a form of racism. Universities began requiring students to take courses highlighting the concept of "white privilege" and funding for academic departments of race and gender studies from the Ford Foundation, Rockefeller think tanks, and other sources significantly increased.

Obama attempted to restore good feelings with the Muslim world and to address the resentments and anger boiling from the African American community about the rising police state. Obama also attempted to stabilize the economy with mild regulations of Wall Street and his "Obamacare" healthcare reform.

It was amid this push-back against Neoconservatism, that Kamala Harris served as San Francisco district attorney from 2004 to 2011. It was in 2011, in a political atmosphere tainted by the Arab spring and the Occupy protests that Kamala Harris became California's State Attorney General. At the time, the African American community had a renewed trust in government institutions due to Obama's ascendency, though it wouldn't last long.

Across Middle America, Tea Party protests were mobilized in which Obama was accused of being a Nazi, Communist, or Muslim. The right wing launched efforts to stop his modest reforms with catastrophic alarmist rhetoric. Obama's reforms were mild at best, but at every turn they were labelled "communist."

The right-wing struggled to reinvent itself as anti-establishment sentiments surged following the financial crisis. On FOX News Channel Glenn Beck began lecturing audiences with McCarthy-era anti-communism, drawing on a chalk board to explain elaborate theories about the influence of Islam, Communism, and George Soros. Libertarianism and non-Neoconservative elements suddenly had the upper hand among Republicans, as the "Late Cold War Normal" had pretty much been broken.

The establishment left also appeared to be confused and unclear about how to move forward. Unrest among African Americans escalated as Obama's presidency continued. The fact that a commander-in-chief of African descent was not improving the situation spurred many African-Americans to protest in places like Ferguson and Baltimore. Rather than resolving racial unrest, Obama's presidency escalated existing tensions and outrage about the police state and mass incarceration.

Meanwhile, despite successfully destroying Libya, in Syria the United States seemed unable to topple the Baath Socialist Government. Russia and China's economic influence around the world was expanding.

While the economy stabilized in the aftermath of the 2008-2009 crash, living standards were continuing to decrease. Opioid addiction and suicide were on the rise and the US life expectancy decreased. Many white Americans felt as if their needs were being ignored while international affairs and the needs of the African-American community took priority.

E. Trump's Reaction

Amid the failures of the Obama administration to calm racial unrest, solve economic problems, or roll back the influence of geopolitical rivals of the United States, Trump emerged with his psuedo-populistic nationalism. Like Nixon he spoke of "law and order" and a "silent majority" and he was hated by many of the Neoconservatives within the Republican Party.

As US society presents itself in a more liberal way, not just domestically but to the world, right-wing ideas have come to represent a perceived opposition to the status quo. Following the decline of Neoconservativism, Libertarians and advocates of Austrian school economics, along with conspiracy theorists, and isolationists have taken more of the center stage among conservatives. What was first manifested with Ron Paul and his longstanding "constitutionalist" opposition to the mainstream of the Republican Party, tied to the John Birch Society and the militia movement, has become more mainstream within the Republican Party. Many Neoconservatives have loudly objected to this and denounced Trump.

Trump sits at the center of a diverse coalition of interests, facing opposition from the highest levels of American capital. His backers include fracking companies, longstanding competitors with the big four super major oil companies. They also include individuals tied to military contractors and weapons manufacturers like Betsy DeVos, his billionaire secretary of education. Bernie Marcus, the owner of Home Depot, strongly backs Trump, as does Nevada real-estate giant Sheldon Adelson.

Trump has attached himself to key hawkish constituencies among the country's foreign exile community. Miami Cubans, exiles from Iran, Netanyahu supporting right-wing Israelis, and admirers of Modi in India all throw their weight behind Trump. The desires of these particular interest groups tend to go against the broader US foreign policy apparatus that thinks in terms of long term global strategy and doesn't share their short term goals and vendettas.

The biggest banks, the four super major oil companies, and the silicon valley tech giants all incarnate a powerful, globally oriented liberal faction that opposes him. They seek to make the USA more racially inclusive and to destabilize anti-imperialist countries in the name of spreading human rights. They favor a more social democratic model perhaps involving universal basic income to stabilize US society, as the population is transitioned to lower living standards across the board. They favor reduction of consumption in the name of fighting global warming, and further integrating the US economy into a global market.

While Trump's faction focuses on increasing its own short term profits, the "globalist" faction that Trump decries focuses on maintaining stability while gradually implementing long term goals. Pouring billions of dollars into research and social engineering, the upper faction of US capital favors gradually and carefully reducing living standards, eliminating anti-imperialist governments around the world, transitioning to a more open global economy, normalizing police state repression in everyday life, and reducing the human population.

The Trump coalition views these powerful forces as "globalists" who are disloyal to the country and seeks to depose them. It blames them for the shortcomings of the Obama administration, for continued economic decline, for failing US foreign policies, and for rising unrest. The Trump movement with its slogans of "America First" is an attempt by the lower levels of American capital to assert its needs against the ultra-rich "progressive" faction.

The pandemic has put these differences pretty clearly on display. Amazon, Wal-Mart, Google, and many of the biggest corporations favored prolonging the lockdown as their profits kept rolling in. Meanwhile, lower level capitalists like the owners of Hobby Lobby who support Trump, or the fracking companies who suffered from a lack of oil demand, saw the pandemic drive them into bankruptcy. The lower level capitalists demanded, successfully, that states open up prematurely for economic reasons, laying the basis for prolonging the high rate of infection. Meanwhile, silicon valley sits at the center of Andrew Cuomo and Bill De Blasio's plans to reinvent New York City in the aftermath of the pandemic.

The Yankee and Cowboy War described by Carl Ogelsby decades ago is still in effect, but it has become much more complicated. The Cold War Liberals have evolved into a sinister group of social engineers, and have gained the upper hand by dominating social media and watching neoconservative strategies and rhetoric become utterly bankrupt. Meanwhile, the pre-neoconservative "old right" of the McCarthy era is back, harnessing anti-establishment sentiments on behalf of lower level capitalists.

* * * * *

Joe Biden and Kamala Harris have positioned themselves to represent the Eastern Establishment, the Rockefeller faction of "progressive" and "globalist" minded bankers, oil companies, and tech giants. They view Trump's misleadership as creating instability, mishandling the pandemic, and weakening the United States internationally in the struggle to roll back the influence of Russia and China.

Kamala Harris, a prosecutor with sadistic tendencies and disregard for the rights of others, who grew up amid the New Left, but rose to power within the neoconservative mass incarceration apparatus, has ascended from US Senator to the position of the Democratic Party's Vice Presidential Nominee.

With Joe Biden appearing quite elderly, amid widespread speculation that he is senile, Harris could easily not only win the Vice Presidency, but become President of the United States. If Biden's condition continues to deteriorate after winning in November, Harris is likely to be taking the oath of office and becoming the first female commander-in-chief within the next four years.

Kamala Harris fits into the trajectory of US politics since WW2. She has been selected to play a particular role, for a particular faction, amid a situation of continued instability and division within the country.

She could soon be president despite being rejected by the voters in the Democratic primary. In this light, the ugly facts about her career history, which are largely being overlooked by mainstream media, are particularly disturbing.

2. Psychology Behind Politics

When examining the life story and personalities of the four most recent US Presidents, striking similarities can be found.

US President Bill Clinton never met his biological father. He was raised by his mother. An alcoholic and abusive stepfather came and went. Bill Clinton discovered at a relatively young age that he had a high amount of charisma in both public speaking and one on one interactions. This charm probably developed from being "mother's little boy" and consoling and entertaining his maternal companion. Furthermore, due to life circumstances, Clinton's mother most likely pushed him and was highly invested in seeing him succeed.

Despite growing up in very different parts of the country (and the world), Barack Obama's life story and personal development path is eerily similar. Obama's biological father separated from his mother when he was a small child. Obama wrote a memoir about how this experience affected him entitled *Dreams from My Father*. Obama was raised by his mother, Ann Dunham, and his grandparents. For a few years Obama and his mother lived with a stepfather who was a leader of the Indonesian military. Many have speculated that domestic violence may have played a role in the separation and divorce of Ann Dunham and Lolo Soetoro, though this allegation is not widely reported as it is in the case of Clinton's stepfather.

Obama's mother had big aspirations for her son, and like Bill Clinton, the young Obama discovered he had a talent for winning people's trust and charming an audience. Both Clinton and Obama came from relatively modest, middle class backgrounds, but moved up through the channels of US society, namely Ivy League Schools, where potential leaders are vetted.

Both of them became two-term US Presidents from the Democratic Party, and both of them were strongly committed to "regime change" operations conducted in the name of "human rights." Both of them developed a style of rhetoric channeling radicals of the past. Bill Clinton evoked memories of southern populists and labor leaders. Barack Obama evoked memories of the civil rights movement.

However, despite their deeply impactful rhetoric, they both delivered fairly moderate and unexciting economic and social policies. They learned the art of being radical and inspirational in tone, while moderate in content. Audiences would be inspired by the radicalism and optimism in their voices, while ignoring the banality of the actual words they spoke. Just as they stood before their mothers as boys, giving them hope in hard times and cheering them on a rainy day, they now stood before America reassuring them with talk of "change you can believe in" or coming from "a little place called Hope."

Meanwhile, Donald Trump and George W. Bush also have shockingly similar life stories. The father of George W. Bush was none other than CIA director, Vice President and eventually President George Herbert Walker Bush. Bush grew up in the household of his highly successful father, viewed as the screw up, the failure, and the disappointing son.

The youthful years of George W. Bush involved struggling with alcoholism and cocaine addiction and performing poorly in academics. But the young "Dubya"" loved to be the life of the party, and seemed to have a very strong desire to win the approval of others. Following his education at elite schools, he was involved in a series of failed business ventures before turning to politics almost as a last resort. To the surprise of his mother and brothers, George W. Bush became governor of Texas and eventually President of the United States. His bumbling malapropisms and almost child-like desire to win the approval of others became a winning attribute, making George W. Bush seem more human and genuine than his rivals.

Donald Trump also had a highly achieving father who viewed him as a disappointment. Trump's father was a wealthy New York City real estate giant, well connected to the inner circles of New York City's political elite. Trump's father sent his teenage son to a military boarding school known for straightening out rebellious young men with harsh discipline.

Trump, of course, had something to prove. He entered adulthood determined not only to make money, but to make a name for himself. Like Bush, Trump spent his youth as the life of the party and seemed to have a desperation for media attention and the approval of others. Like George W. Bush, Trump engaged in a series of grandiose yet failed business ventures before ultimately turning to politics. Trump, like Bush, became appreciated for his poor use of the English language. This made him seem more average and less manufactured than standard politicians. The crassness and impoliteness of his words also won him admiration and media attention.

Bush was known for his Texas accent, his improper grammar, and his pushing of the envelope when it came to authoritarianism. He spoke of fighting terrorists like a cowboy movie, saying he would "smoke 'em out" and defended the use of torture. Trump is known for making wildly factually inaccurate statements, as well as wildly self aggrandizing ones. His rhetorical style includes giving demeaning nicknames to his political rivals, and emphasizing how "tough" he is. Trump has called for killing the family members of suspected terrorists, and also saying that he believes in torture.

Barack Obama and Bill Clinton are certainly not clones. Neither are Trump and George W. Bush. However, their life stories and family histories are eerily similar and this fact should certainly raise the eyebrows of anyone who has studied personality theory.

The position of US President is vitally important to setting the course of global events. The ability to influence the person in such a position, push their buttons, motivate them to take certain actions and prevent them from taking others, is vitally important. Billions of dollars and millions of lives are often on the line. The fact that similar personalities have occupied the oval office for the past few decades is not accidental, or merely the natural workings of our political system. One can be sure that the personality of each potential POTUS is heavily studied from a number of different angles, by different forces that seek to push them in one direction or another.

The rise of Kamala Harris must be understood in this context. What is her family background? How has it impacted her career trajectory? When discussing someone who was rejected by Democratic Primary voters, but is likely to soon have her finger on the nuclear button, it becomes an important question.

"That Little Girl Was Me"

On the debate stage during the Democratic Primary in June of 2019, Kamala Harris often clashed with Joe Biden. Biden and Bernie Sanders were the top two candidates favored among democratic voters, and Kamala wanted to secure her position in the race. While Kamala clashed with other candidates, memories of her pre-adolescent childhood were invoked far more frequently than is usual for politicians.

"Growing up my sister and I had to deal with the neighbor, who told us her parents said they couldn't play with us because we were Black," she told the millions who watched the debate on CNN.

When she went after Joe Biden, her rhetoric got even more personal: "I'm going to now direct this at Vice President Biden. I do not believe you are a racist. I agree with you when you commit yourself to the importance of finding common ground…I also believe … It's personal. It was actually hurtful to hear you talk about the reputations of two United States senators who built their reputations and career on the segregation of race in this country… It was not only that but you also worked with them to oppose busing. There was a little girl in California who was part of the second class to integrate her public schools. She was bused to school every day. That little girl was me."

These were not accidental or unplanned remarks, as almost immediately afterward her campaign website began offering T-shirts with photographs of Kamala Harris as a small child, with her hair in braids. The phrase "That Little Girl Was Me" was immediately all over twitter. The photo and phrase had been a planned meme for marketing Kamala Harris.

However, it points to the fact that Kamala Harris deeply identifies with her pre-adolescent self, and feelings associated with her childhood are a primary motivation for her behavior, right up to the present day. The "little girl" that Kamala Harris invokes and the strong emotions attached to it underly many of her actions.

This theme can be consistently observed throughout her political career. In 2010, Kamala Harris spoke before the Commonwealth Club of California. A disturbing clip from these remarks has become widely circulated, showing a side of Kamala Harris which her campaign would most likely prefer to conceal. In the clip, Kamala boasts that she jailed the parents of truant school kids and laughs about it.

"Well, this was a little controversial in San Francisco," she says with a big grin on her face, before breaking into a cackle of sadistic laughter. "Frankly, my staff went bananas, they were concerned because they didn't know at the time whether I was going to have an opponent in the election."

She went on to describe the feelings of power she felt in her position after taking it: "As a prosecutor and law enforcement, I have a huge stick, the school district has got a carrot, let's work in tandem around our collective objective and goal, to get those kids in school." She went on to giggle about a parent showing a letter from the district attorney's office to her children and saying "If you don't go to school Kamala is going to put you and me in jail."

Most viewers are disturbed by the fact that Kamala Harris seems to relish having a "big stick" and being able to punish low income people. The jailing of low-income parents for their children's truancy is unlikely to improve their life circumstances. The fact that Kamala boasts that she rushed to implement this policy as soon as she came into office is equally disturbing.

However, the most telling statement in the clips comes just prior to Kamala describing her harsh actions. Kamala stated: "I would not be standing here were it not for the education I received, and I know many of us would say the same thing. I believe a child going without an education is tantamount to a crime, so I decided I was going to start prosecuting parents for truancy."

We see this common pattern in her rhetoric. Kamala Harris invokes her own childhood, and how she "would not be standing here" if her parents had not sent her to school, in order to justify her actions. She goes on to boast about how she felt after taking office; she had enough "capital" to take this dramatic move, despite the political risks. She speaks of her "big stick," she giggles with delight about how upset her staff was with her decision. She speaks of parents sending their kids to school out of fear of incarceration, and how delighted she felt about sending a letter with a District Attorney's badge on the letterhead to parents throughout the Bay Area.

So, why does Kamala seem to invoke childhood memories so much? Why is a woman who is well over 50 years old constantly invoking her life situation during the late 1960s and early 1970s?

Meet Donald Harris

In February of 2019, Donald Harris, the father of Kamala Harris, opened up about his daughter and her Presidential campaign. He was infuriated because Kamala Harris had stated "half my family is from Jamaica, are you kidding me?" when asked if she had smoked marijuana.

Donald's words were harsh: "My dear departed grandmothers... as well as my deceased parents, must be turning in their grave right now to see their family's name, reputation, and proud Jamaican identity being connected, in any way jokingly or not, with the fraudulent stereotype of a pot-smoking joy seeker and in the pursuit of identity politics. Speaking for myself and my immediate Jamaican family, we wish to categorically dissociate ourselves from this travesty."

Donald Harris is an economics professor, now retired with emeritus status from Stanford University. To describe Donald Harris as a "Communist" is a bit of an exaggeration. He is certainly heavily influenced by Marx's economic theories in his analysis of unemployment and GDP growth. His writings certainly discuss concepts such as overproduction, the falling rate of profit, and the general law of capitalist accumulation, and apply them when explaining and predicting trends.

Donald Harris taught economics at Stanford University, drawing heavily from Marxism. He also served as an economic advisor to various Prime Ministers of Jamaica.

However, Donald Harris is not a left-wing agitator or even really an activist. In addition to teaching courses at Stanford University, Harris served as an economic advisor to three Jamaican prime ministers. Social-democracy and the "labourite" political tradition certainly has a lot of influence in Jamaica. Michael Manley served as prime minister from 1972 to 1980, and from 1989 to 1992. Manley called himself a Democratic Socialist and enacted many progressive reforms, including the creation of free healthcare clinics, rent and price controls, and subsidies of food for low income people.

Donald Harris seems to have functioned not as a political strategist, agitator, or commentator, but as a policy formulator and an interpreter of economic data, giving advice to Jamaican elected officials behind the scenes. He most likely had significant influence within the administrations of a number of prime ministers, who struggled to increase living standards and stabilize the impoverished Caribbean country.

Aside from his denunciation of his daughter's statements about Jamaica, a short essay entitled "Reflections of a Jamaican Father," Donald Harris has so far been mostly silent about his daughter, and intends to remain so. However, the essay in which Harris reflects on his upbringing is quite revealing, and provides us with some insights into what underlying motivations lay beneath Kamala's words and actions.

Donald Harris writes, regarding his two estranged daughters: "My one big regret is that they did not come to know very well the two most influential women in my life: "Miss Chrishy" and "Miss Iris" (as everybody called them). This is, in many ways, a story about these women and the heritage they gave us. My roots go back, within my lifetime, to my paternal grandmother Miss Chrishy (née Christiana Brown, descendant of Hamilton Brown who is on record as plantation and slave owner and founder of Brown's Town), and to my maternal grandmother Miss Iris (née Iris Finegan, farmer and educator, from Aenon Town and Inverness, ancestry unknown to me). The Harris name comes from my paternal grandfather Joseph Alexander Harris, land-owner and agricultural 'produce' exporter (mostly pimento or all-spice), who died in 1939 one year after I was born and is buried in the church yard of the magnificent Anglican Church which Hamilton Brown built in Brown's Town (and where, as a child, I learned the catechism, was baptized and confirmed, and served as an acolyte). Both of my grandmothers had the strongest influence on my early upbringing ("not to exclude, of course, the influence of my dear mother 'Miss Beryl' and loving father 'Maas Oscar')."

Harris reflects on the influence of "Miss Chrishy" on his trajectory toward studying economics: "There was a daily diet of politics as well. She was a great admirer of 'Busta' (Sir William Alexander Bustamante, then Chief Minister in the colonial government and leader of the Jamaica Labour Party (JLP)). She claimed, with conviction and pride, to be a "Labourite" (as members of the JLP were called), and for the interesting reason that, as she argued, "labour is at the heart of everything in life". Little did I know then, what I learned later in studying economics, that my grandmother was espousing her independently discovered version of a Labour Theory of Value!"

"The Adventurous and Assertive One"

Harris tells a touching anecdote about his two daughters, and subtly hinting at Kamala's character as a child: "Now, far away in the diaspora in 2018, one of the most vivid and fondest memories I have of that early period with my children is of the visit we made in 1970 to Orange Hill. We trudged through the cow dung and rusted iron gates, up-hill and down-hill, along narrow unkempt paths, to the very end of the family property, all in my eagerness to show to the girls the terrain over which I had wandered daily for hours as a boy (with Miss Chrishy hollering in the distance: "yu better cum home now, bwoy, or else!"). Upon reaching the top of a little hill that opened much of that terrain to our full view, Kamala, ever the adventurous and assertive one, suddenly broke from the pack, leaving behind Maya the more cautious one, and took off like a gazelle in Serengeti, leaping over rocks and shrubs and fallen branches, in utter joy and unleashed curiosity, to explore that same enticing terrain. I quickly followed her with my trusted *Canon Super Eight* movie camera to record the moment (in my usual role as cameraman for every occasion). I couldn't help thinking there and then: What a moment of exciting *re*discovery being handed over from one generation to another!"

His reference to Kamala as "ever the adventurous and assertive one" seems to indicate that these are character traits the VP nominee had in her childhood which have carried over into adulthood. One can detect a tone of bittersweet sadness in these memories of Kamala's estranged father. Donald Harris is reflecting on the character of his now world famous daughter at the age of 6 in 1970, before she was swept out of his life by a divorce that was likely far more ugly than Kamala wants the world to know.

Harris writes: "This early phase of interaction with my children came to an abrupt halt in 1972 when, after a hard-fought custody battle in the family court of Oakland, California, the context of the relationship was placed within arbitrary limits imposed by a court-ordered divorce settlement based on the false assumption by the State of California that fathers cannot handle parenting (especially in the case of this father, "a neegroe from da eyelans" was the Yankee stereotype, who might just end up eating his children for breakfast!). Nevertheless, I persisted, never giving up on my love for my children or reneging on my responsibilities as their father. So, here we are now."

Donald's words about family court in Oakland, completely contradicts the presentation of events found in Kamala's autobiography. Kamala writes about her parents separation: "They didn't fight about money. The only thing they fought about was who got the books."

It is pretty apparent that her parents fought about a few other things; namely, who got custody over Kamala and her younger sister. The fact that Kamala chose to conceal this in her autobiography could be very telling.

In another passage, Kamala reflects on her parents' relationship with carefully chosen words: "I've often thought that had they been a little older, more emotionally mature, maybe the marriage could have survived. But they were so young. My father was my mother's first boyfriend." The implication of this fact about her mother's lack of a dating history prior to her marriage could be read as presenting her mother as young and naive, or could instead be interpreted to present her father as predatory. The implication is carefully left to the reader.

None of this would be worth discussing, if not for the fact that Kamala Harris speaks of her childhood excessively. The implication of some of her statements is that we are almost expected to vote for her simply out of sympathy for the suffering she endured as a 10-year-old. Sympathy for ethnic minority children and the very real hardships they have endured in times past and still endure across the country is a quite important theme in the rhetoric of identity politics. Many Black activists, for example, argued that they voted for Barack Obama simply so their children could grow up with the self-esteem of knowing it was possible for them to be president.

Kamala's constant invoking of her childhood could simply be about marketing herself in the age of what detractors refer to as "IDPOL." But other aspects of the biographical narrative put out by Kamala's staff and supporters are worth noting. In addition to the references to her childhood, the Harris campaign has done a lot to almost canonize her now deceased mother. Shyamala Gopalan is presented as a feminist pioneer, immigrating from India, getting her degree, and becoming a cancer researcher. Photos of Shymala have been tweeted out. Anecdotes about her have come up in Kamala's speeches.

However, Kamala Harris and her campaign are pretty silent in regard to her father. He receives no such cannonization, despite also being an immigrant and a man of color who met her mother through left-wing activism. The fact that Donald says he lost his ability to really interact with his daughters in 1972 and that he has denounced her in the press indicates that the relationship between them is weak at best. The harshness of Donald's words, referring to Kamala's campaign as a "travesty" and engaging in "pursuit of identity politics" certainly stands out. Have the relatives of any potential US Presidents in recent years spoken so harshly?

What is the source of this obvious tension and weak relationship between Kamala Harris and her father? Other than the divorce, we really do not know. We can only speculate.

In Donald's essay reflecting on his Jamaican upbringing and his relationship with his own daughters, he describes his paternal grandmother and speaks in a positive tone about her use of corporal punishment. Harris writes: "Miss Chrishy was the disciplinarian, reserved and stern in look, firm with 'the strap', but capable of the most endearing and genuine acts of love, affection, and care."

Corporal punishment is widely practiced among Jamaicans and Jamaican Americans even today. In 2020, school teachers in Jamaica are still known to spank or beat their students though officially urged not to do so by the Ministry of Education. The British colonial tradition of "six of the best" canings is something that remains part of life for schoolchildren in many parts of the developing world. Jamaica maintained the practice of sentencing juvenile offenders and other criminals to floggings with a "tamarind switch" until 1998. Many Jamaican legislators have proposed this punishment method be revived as an alternative to jail, and received lots of public support in their call.

Did Donald Harris beat his daughters? Does Kamala resent him because of this? This is certainly possible. In the 1960s and 70s, corporal punishment of children was far more widely accepted, and was nearly expected among both families and schools in the United States across almost all strata of society. Dr. Spock's best-selling book urging parents to refrain from this traditional disciplinary practice was often mocked and rejected. Even today, 19 US states allow teachers in public schools to beat students with wooden paddles.

However, the liberal activist and academic environment which Kamala's parents inhabited would most likely have frowned on such methods of childrearing, so this is quite unclear. Is it possible her parents disagreed in regard to how young Kamala and her sister were disciplined?

The fixation on vengeful "justice" and punishment that defines Kamala's adult life would certainly fit the profile of one who had experienced harsh beatings as a child. However, in times past in which extreme corporal punishment was fairly common, many grew into adulthood having experienced harsh corporal punishment without the sadistic tendencies Kamala Harris displays.

Perhaps the resentment is rooted in other aspects of her parent's separation. The split between Kamala's parents was clearly not a friendly one. What was the "immaturity" Kamala blames for the failure of her parents marriage? What prompted the divorce? Was there an extra-marital affair? Was there domestic violence? Is it possible that young Kamala observed her father striking her mother?

We do not know the answer to these questions. Is it perhaps possible that Donald Harris was nothing but a gentle, patient, loving father? Could it be that Kamala's family experienced financial hardships following the divorce, as two children were raised by a single mother? Did Shymala perhaps scapegoat her ex-husband and raise Kamala and her sister to believe he was responsible for the problems of their household?

Much has been written about the painful effects of what is called "Parental Child Abduction and Alienation" where in divorce proceedings, children are pulled away from one parent and incited against them. This is not done out a pure intention of protecting the children, but out of a selfish parent's desire to spite and punish the other parent.

Did Kamala perhaps learn to overlook her mother's shortcomings and channel her frustrations with their life onto a "dead beat dad" from "da eyelans'? Donald's essay hints that he is coming from a defensive place and that perhaps his responsibleness as a father has been questioned. In

Donald's public denunciation of his daughter, it becomes clear that stereotypes of Jamaicans as lazy, pot smoking, irresponsible, and not good fathers get under his skin more than anything else. Did young Kamala observe her mother pushing these buttons to evoke her father's rage? Did her mother adopt this narrative about her father presenting him as such a stereotype to her daughters in the aftermath of the divorce?

There is certainly deep pain of some sort underlying Kamala's cruelty. The estrangement from her father is likely to be a major source of such pain. In *The Truths We Hold,* while Kamala clearly has glossed over much of the pain of her upbringing, on a few occasions she reveals inner damage beneath the surface. Describing her high school commencement ceremony she writes: "I invited both of my parents to come to my graduation, even though I knew they wouldn't speak to each other. I still wanted them both to be there for me. I'll never forget sitting in the first couple of rows of the auditorium, looking out at the audience. My mother was nowhere to be found. 'Where is she?' I thought. 'Is she not here because my father is?'… Then all of the sudden, the back door of the auditorium opened up and my mother… walked in wearing a bright red dress and heels. She was never one to let the situation get the better of her."

In this anecdote, once again Shymala is the hero. The fact that her mother might be so afraid of her seeing Donald Harris that she would potentially skip her daughter's commencement ceremony almost a decade later, indicates more than mere bad feelings about a failed marriage.

Whether Kamala Harris was aware of it or not, when she destroyed the lives of pot smokers, withheld evidence to convict people, blocked exonerations, and jailed low income parents, she was not protecting the innocent or sticking up for the downtrodden. Putting the parents of low income truant children in jail

often results in pushing them into the foster care system. The results of breaking apart families is tragic.

As a result of her many actions as a rising star in California's prosecutorial school-to-prison pipeline apparatus, getting "tough on crime" and pushing for harsh sentences, countless thousands of children grew up like her, without their father. Kamala's use of her cherished "big stick" to tear apart families, the actions she cackles about, did not really benefit children.

It seems that the "little girl" who Kamala frequently invokes, the one who probably once felt powerless and afraid, is seeking to exact revenge. The actual results for actual people are irrelevant. As the image of 10 year old Kamala flickers in her mind, a rage that has burned for decades continues to be kindled. No matter how many lives are destroyed, the world must be made to understand "that little girl was me."

The Destructive Impulse

Much like the similarities between Obama and Clinton, Trump and Bush, Kamala's life story is all too similar to many other prominent female political figures. Amy Klobuchar, the US Senator from Minnesota who also ran in the 2020 Democratic Presidential primary, has a similar biography. She was raised by a mother after a divorce. In her case, we know there was domestic violence, with her alcoholic father beating her mother. Like Kamala, Amy was estranged from her father until he became sober decades later. Amy Klobuchar became a criminal prosecutor in the same era, and utilized the same fear mongering tactics, filling prisons in Minnesota with low income African American men.

Samantha Power, the UN ambassador under Barack Obama who worked inside the White House pushing for the Libyan intervention, shares a similar life story. Power was born in Ireland. When Samantha Power was 9 years old, she moved to the United States with her mother. Power and her mother left behind their father, who died of an alcohol induced illness a few years later.

Kamala Harris, Amy Klobuchar, and Samantha Power have dedicated their lives to punishing and destroying. Harris and Klobuchar destroyed the lives of low income, mostly Black men in court rooms, and rose up in the ranks due to the enthusiasm with which they carried out this task, ensuring huge profits for the prison industrial complex.

Samantha Power dedicated her life to building the case, not for the incarceration of individuals, but for the military destruction of nations. In her book, *Problem From Hell: America and the Age of Genocide,* Power wrote that the US government: "needed help from American reporters, editorial boards, and advocacy groups" in order to convince the world about the need to ruthlessly bomb and destabilize former Yugoslavia.

Just as a fishmonger sells fish, Samantha Power sold war. She pushed for the bombing of Yugoslavia, the destruction of Libya, and defended efforts to destabilize Syria. Similar to Kamala Harris' jailing of truant children, the results did not improve people's lives. Millions of Serbians, Syrians, and Libyans were killed, had their homes destroyed, or were forced to become refugees. But to Samantha Power, it wasn't about helping people, but punishing people. Just like how Kamala's imprisoning of low-income parents did not really help their truant school children.

Not surprisingly, Samantha Power built the case for war against regimes that was led by a powerful male figure, deemed to be a "dictator" in western press. Samantha Power has spent her adult life building the case for military interventions and covert operations to remove "strongmen" who lead governments and often have a somewhat fatherly public persona. Muammar Gaddaffi actually referred to Barack Obama as his "little African son."

It is easy to speculate that in the psyche of Kamala Harris, the parents of truant children, and the various African-American males she convicted are psychological stand-ins for a dark-skinned father against whom she has a high amount of rage.

Of course, none of this can be certain. In each of these life histories of President and political figures, there are undoubtedly countless unknown factors driving their career choices and personality development. Biological factors like brain chemistry, the influence of religion, the personality of influential teachers, mentors, and childhood friends all can have immeasurable impact on how the human mind and personality develops. Books like *The Truths We Hold* which are published by politicians aspiring for the Presidency are often carefully edited in order to market the candidate.

In generations past, many Americans grew up hearing a story of George Washington admitting to cutting down his father's cherry tree because he "cannot tell a lie." The story is now universally recognized to be fictional propaganda intended to moralize schoolchildren in the generations after Washington's death. While technology and accessibility of information have certainly changed since the early years of the United States, the dishonest nature of personality cults and political leaders has not. Everything in Kamala's memoirs and speeches and in her father's reflections should be taken with a "grain of salt."

If Kamala Harris ends up being Vice President, or President, we will learn infinitely more about her character as it is on display before the world. We will see what Kamala has to offer, not just in terms of words but also in terms of concrete policy that can impact the lives of potentially billions of people.

The Revolutionary Intelligentsia

This impulse to destroy and tear things down was a key factor in the bourgeois revolutions to overthrow feudalism and establish the liberal societies around which the global economy is now centered. In 1804, the English poet William Blake composed these verses to celebrate sentiments of the age when nation states and democratic republics were established as kings fell amid revolutionary bloodbaths. Blake wrote:

> *Bring me my bow of burning gold!*
> *Bring me my arrows of desire!*
> *Bring me my spear, oh clouds unfold!*
> *Bring me my chariot of fire!*
> *I will not cease from mental fight,*
> *Nor shall my sword sleep in my hand*
> *Til we have built Jerusalem*
> *In England's green and pleasant land.*

As these words were written, the world was still reacting to the dramatic events in France during the previous decade. The monarchy had been toppled and a republic had been established. A "reign of terror" involving mass executions of nobles, priests, and individuals deemed to be contrary to the French revolution's values had taken place. The guillotine, now used as a class struggle emblem by some young liberal "democratic socialists" was used to behead thousands of people in a carnival like atmosphere.

The French Revolution involved the active deconstruction, not only of the feudal economic and political order, but the mindset that went along with it. Peasants who had been forbidden from even looking nobles in the eye and had been forced to bow and obey in almost every aspect of life were suddenly given permission to unleash their rage. This explosion of rage shook all of society and enabled the capitalists to take power from feudal aristocrats.

Previously restrained sexual impulses were also unleashed. The Marquis De Sade, the pornographic French writer from whom the term "sadism" is derived, was a key figure in the French revolution. Sade had been imprisoned at the Bastille for his sexual assaults and other anti-social behaviors. From inside the prison, he had screamed out of the windows to the crowds on the streets of Paris that prisoners inside were being tortured and cruelly treated. Sensing that the Marquis was agitating Parisians and potentially causing unrest, the jailers transferred him to a mental hospital outside of the city. 10 days after the Marquis de Sade was removed from the infamous prison, mobs of revolutionaries stormed it on July 14, 1789. The "Storming of the Bastille" is considered an iconic moment in French history, celebrated with a national holiday.

The Marquis de Sade's role in the French Revolution was not limited to agitation from prison windows. Sade was a keynote speaker at the funeral of Jacobin agitator Jean-Paul Marat, giving a glowing eulogy. For the Marquis de Sade, sexuality and violence were closely linked to each other, and the unleashing of both signified the liberation of mankind. Indeed, the unleashing of passion and rage was key in bringing down feudalism. As a result of the French revolution, it has become an almost permanent attribute of leftist politics as it developed.

The terms "Left" and "Right" actually originated in the French National Assembly formed amid revolutionary upheaval. Those loyal to the King sat on the right, while the radicals and advocates of "Liberte, Egalite, Fraternite" sat on the left.

Sigmund Freud, the founder of psychoanalysis, wrote that renegotiating the restraints imposed by society on the natural impulses of individuals toward violence and sex is a key factor underlying many political conflicts throughout history. Freud wrote: "The liberty of the individual is no gift to civilization...The development of civilization imposes restriction on it, and justice demands that no one escape those restrictions. What makes itself felt in a human community as a desire for freedom may be their revolt against some existing injustice and so many prove favorable to further development of civilization; it may remain compatible with civilization. But it may also spring from the remains of their original personality, which is still untamed by civilization and thus may be the basis in them for hostility to civilization. The urge for freedom, therefore, is directed against particular forms and demands of civilization or against civilization altogether. It does not seem that any influence could induce a man to change his nature into a termite's. No doubt he will defend his claim of individual liberty against the will of the group... A good part of the struggles of mankind centre round the single task of finding an expedient accommodation — one, that is, that will bring happiness — between the claims of the individual and cultural claims of the group; and one of the problems that touches the fate of humanity is whether such an accommodation can be reached by some particular form of civilization or whether this conflict is irreconcilable."

The French Revolution gave birth to a tendency of modern capitalist societies that can be rightly called "the revolutionary intelligentsia." These are intellectuals, students, artists, writers, and activists who feel alienated from society and seek to build a new world. These "bohemians" or "radicals" existed across Europe in the 1800s, and now exist in almost every country in the world. It is a middle class current, in which youth are significantly represented.

Karl Marx and Frederich Engels were among this strata, debating with other "Left Hegelians" in the cafes of Paris and London. Marxism emerged as the dominant current among the students and intellectuals of Europe, who felt the bourgeois revolutions had failed to deliver a truly just society, and that "building Jerusalem" required further storming of barricades and firing of rifles.

While conservatives throughout Europe sought to reinforce religion, patriarchy, and tradition, the organized political left became associated with lifting restraints on human impulses. The Marxists generally sought to come to power by giving workers permission to be angry at their bosses, giving women permission to be angry about traditional gender roles, giving youth permission to be angry at authority, and combining this anger into a gigantic social explosion in which the revolutionaries could take power. This was the method of the French revolution, and throughout Europe it was quite effective.

Karl Marx participated in the 1848 German Revolution, as did Frederich Nietschze and Richard Wagner. The unleashing of passion was certainly evident in the 1848 events as peasants marched off to battle singing "Duetschland, Deutschland, Uber Alles!" in the hopes of toppling the local nobles and aristocrats and uniting the various territories into a modern nation state governed by a democratic republic. The failure of the 1848 revolution resulted in a mass exodus from Germany by the socialists, radicals, and religious fanatics who had fought on the front lines.

The various Marxist revolutionaries of the 20th century, Lenin, Trotsky, Mao, Castro, Guevara, and others originated among the revolutionary intelligentsia as wealthy students who studied revolutionary ideas and sought to remake the world around them. Many of them learned how to effectively unleash the rage of peasants, workers, and students against the semi-feudal systems of the developing world and utilized the unleashing of passions in order to take power. Mao Zedong, for example, knew very well how to tap into the anger of peasants against landlords, as well as the anger of youth at China's highly traditional Confucian family structure. Rage at the old regime was very visible in the immediate aftermath of the Russian Revolution with the destruction of churches. The large number of executions of figures from the Batista regime in the early years of the Cuban Revolution harnessed similar anger.

The Emergence of Constructive Socialism

However, when Communists have taken power they hold onto power by appealing to very different emotions. The strength of the Soviet Union was not that it gave permission to individuals to unleash their rage, but rather that it provided a sense of community and joint effort that enabled the country to be rapidly industrialized.

The PBS documentary film *Red Flag 1917* produced after the fall of the Soviet Union featured interviews with Tatiana Fedorova. As a youth, Tatiana had been a leader of construction projects during Stalin's Five Year Plans to industrialize the Soviet Union. The full transcript of her interview has been published online.

Fedorova described the feelings of building the USSR into an industrial superpower: "Remember, people were illiterate, lived in virtual darkness, wore birch bark shoes. Even now I think it's like something out of a fairy tale. It was one of the most difficult times to build this country. To build these great construction sites would only be possible through unity, the unity of the people and the love of the people to their idol. Stalin for us was an idol."

The five year economic plans of the Soviet Union were viewed with wonder by the entire world. While capitalism was having a great depression, the Soviet Union was being transformed into an industrial superpower. Illiteracy was wiped out. The entire country was electrified and provided

With a mass mobilization of the population around Five Year Plans, the Soviet Union went from being a deeply impoverished country to being an industrial superpower.

with running water. A modern agricultural system with tractors was constructed, as was a modern steel and oil refining industry. With socialist central planning the Soviet Union was able to build itself up into an industrial society that defeated the Nazi invaders and launched the first spacecraft into orbit.

Fedorova went on to describe the experience of building the Moscow subways: "Everyone was trying to do the best for the country, to raise the heights of the motherland. Then there was what we were doing underground...with the Moscow metro. We worked in such a friendly way. It was such a good time. There wasn't so much to eat, we weren't well dressed. We were simply very happy. Happy because we were making it our personal contribution."

When asked about her proudest moment, she said: "It was when the first train went by. It was when the noise of the motor of the first train went by in this clean tunnel which had, until then, only seen the ordinary little carriages. You can't compare that feeling to anything. The construction workers who felt that will feel it forever.... No one forced us to do it. We didn't have to do it, but everyone wanted to... It's very hard to explain but it was the time of the enthusiasts. At that time Mayakovsky said that communism is the young people of the world and we were the young people of those years. Each of us tried to build a foundation of the structures with great joy. It was like a happy song."

When the interviewers from PBS pressed her about the Moscow trials and great terror, asking if they tarnished her faith in socialism she said, "No. No because it was one thing, some political events which happened, and happen in every country -- opposition and so forth. It was a different matter that the country was going on its way at its own speed. People were working. We're talking about a country of many millions. The whole population of the country worked, lived, studied, and sang songs. It doesn't mean that everything was extinguished or everything was lost, no… It was a dark stain. It was a dark stain, but I'll repeat once more that the country was working. All the enterprises were working. The factories were working, children were studying at schools… The fact that these political intrigues and games happened is very unfortunate. It was a very hard time but the country was growing and growing at great speed. There was great power."

The transformation of China from being "the sick man of Asia" to the status of the second largest economy on earth, lifting 800 million from poverty, has been equally inspiring, and equally based on a sense of community and cooperation. Cuba's medical system that sends volunteers across the world, the mobilizations for construction and relief that enabled Hugo Chavez to become very popular in 1999 and defeat the 2002 coup attempt, all drew heavily from this sense of solidarity and optimism.

Figures like Edgar Snow, William Hinton, and Anna Louise Strong visited socialist countries. They reported on the ability of communists to effectively defeat fascist invaders and mobilize the population, often comparing it to early Christianity. The Communists were able to unleash a sense of brotherhood and community that was powerful enough to raise millions from poverty and defeat imperialist attacks.

Across the planet, one can see the great construction projects and achievements carried out by Communists and socialists in the developing world:

- The world's largest irrigation system was constructed by the Islamic Socialist Government of Libya.

- The Dnieper Dam, constructed in the Soviet Union's first five year plan, was the largest hydroelectric power plant in the world at the time it was completed in 1931. It brought electricity to Ukraine and other parts of the Soviet Union.
- The largest power plant in the Middle East, the Aswan Dam, constructed by the Arab Socialist Leader Abdul Nasser, in coordination with the Soviet Union, brought electricity to all of Egypt.
- The China-Pakistan Friendship Highway is one of the longest and highest elevated roadways on earth. It was built by Chinese Communists determined to free their country from the economic isolation that followed the Sino-Soviet split. The highway laid the basis for the origins of the now flourishing China-Pakistan Economic Corridor.
- The Soviet Space Program was the result of the combined heroic efforts of millions of people in the aftermath of the Second World War. It was socialist central planning that launched the first satellites, and put the first person into orbit.
- The Cuban Healthcare System is widely described as one of the greatest in the world. Cuba's medical school that trains doctors from other countries is also widely praised.
- The largest hydroelectric power plant in the world today is the Three Gorges Dam in China, built as part of the Communist Party's efforts to reduce poverty and increase living standards in rural areas.

Many more examples could be given. The achievements of socialism are vast, but the achievements were not conducted on the basis of unleashing anger and seeking punitive revenge. The achievements of socialism were the results of mass mobilizations of the population in a spirit of collectivism.

Across Eastern Europe communists led the reconstruction efforts following the Second World War, paving roads, building hospitals, and raising countries to a higher level of industrialization and living standards than they had ever experienced. The post-war years in Romania, Bulgaria, Poland, Czechoslovakia, Hungary, and other countries liberated by Soviet troops from Nazi invaders are remembered as years of great optimism.

Following the Second World War, the Soviet Union pushed Communist, anti-imperialist and democratic youth groups around the world to establish the World Democratic Youth Federation. Young people from many different countries, who had seen the carnage of war, took this pledge:

> *We pledge that we shall remember this unity, forged in this month, November 1945*
> *Not only today, not only this week, this year, but always*
> *Until we have built the world we have dreamed of and fought for*
> *We pledge ourselves to build the unity of youth of the world*
> *All races, all colors, all nationalities, all beliefs*
> *To eliminate all traces of fascism from the earth*
> *To build a deep and sincere international friendship among the peoples of the world*
> *To keep a just lasting peace*
> *To eliminate want, frustration, and enforced idleness*
> *We have come to confirm the unity of all youth salute our comrades who have died-and pledge our word that skillful hands, keen brains, and young enthusiasm shall never more be wasted in war.*

Every four years a World Festival of Youth and Students was convened by socialist, communist, anti-imperialist, and anti-fascist youth in order to encourage this spirit of human solidarity and unity.

The World Festival of Youth and Students, a tradition started by the Soviet Union in the aftermath of the Second World War.

"Many Wonders and Signs"

In the early years of the Soviet Union, the Communist Party had an internal debate about the way forward. The country was still recovering from a horrendous civil war. Millions of people had died when 15 different countries invaded the Soviet Union in the hopes of overturning the socialist revolution.

Stalin favored a program of "Socialism in one country" while Trotsky proposed a program of "Permanent Revolution." In essence, Stalin sought to appeal to the collective desires of the Soviet peoples for a better life, while Trotsky sought to continue to unleash rage and vengeance, striving for a global revolutionary conflagration. The peoples of the Soviet Union were weary of war, and Trotsky's program of militarizing the life of factory workers and peasants was unappealing to the population, though many hardline Bolsheviks were mistakenly attached to it.

Speaking on January 25, 1921, Stalin criticized the "Permanent Revolution" concept saying: "A group of Party workers headed by Trotsky, intoxicated by the successes achieved by military methods in the army, supposes that those methods can, and must, be adopted among the workers, in the trade unions, in order to achieve similar successes in strengthening the unions and in reviving industry. But this group forgets that the army and the working class are two different spheres, that a method that is suitable for the army may prove to be unsuitable, harmful, for the working class and its trade unions." (Once Again on the Trade Unions, 1921)

Joseph Stalin, a mass organizer who had been educated in a seminary, was known for appealing to quite different sentiments among the people. Long before the Bolshevik revolution, Trotsky had observed this aspect of Stalin with scorn. Historian Simon Sebag Montefiore writes in his biography *Young Stalin* about the organizing style of Russia's future "Man of Steel": "The workers listened reverently to this young preacher — and it was no coincidence that many of the revolutionaries were seminarists, and the workers often pious ex-peasants… Trotsky, agitating in another city, remembered that many of the workers thought the movement resembled the early Christians and had to be taught that they should be atheists."

Montefiore describes how the Bolshevik leader became highly popular when locked in prison alongside non-political criminals: "Stalin was soon the Kingpin of Batumi prison, dominating his friends, terrorizing the intellectuals, suborning the guards and befriending the criminals… Stalin was hostile to bumptious intellectuals, but he was less with the less educated worker-revolutionaries, who did not arouse his inferiority complex, he played the teacher — the priest."

Trotsky and western intellectuals who favored a "permanent revolution" and incarnated the mindset of the revolutionary intelligentsia viewed the industrialization of the USSR with disgust. They denounced Stalin as socially conservative, conducting a "thermidor in the family" and then saw the moment when the population was mobilized to construct as the USSR becoming a "degenerate worker state."

However, the words of Tatiana Fedorova and the millions of other Soviet people who saw their homeland built into an industrial fortress that was strong enough to eventually withstand a fascist invasion tell a different story. In contemporary Russia, Stalin is far more popular than Lenin. Many anti-communists look up to Stalin for his building up of the country.

When Stalin built the Mausoleum for Lenin, and declared the ideology of the Communist Party to be "Marxism-Leninism", many noted the Orthodox religious influence on the propaganda of the new state. Speaking at Lenin's memorial meeting, Stalin spoke of Communists, not as chaos creators, executioners, or vandals, but as a group of people dedicated to living selflessly for the purpose of reinventing mankind: "Comrades, we Communists are people of a special mould. We are made of a special stuff. We are those who form the army of the great proletarian strategist, the army of Comrade Lenin. There is nothing higher than the honor of belonging to this army. There is nothing higher than the title of member of the Party whose founder and leader was Comrade Lenin. It is not given to everyone to be a member of such a party. It is the sons of the working class, the sons of want and struggle, the sons of incredible privation and heroic effort who before all should be members of such a party. That is why the Party of the Leninists, the Party of the Communists, is also called the Party of the working class." (On The Death of Lenin, 1924)

In his text *Civilization and Its Discontents*, Sigmund Freud speaks with contempt for feelings his religious friends describe to him. He writes: "It is a feeling which he would like to call a sensation of 'eternity', a feeling as of something limitless and unbounded - as it were, oceanic. This feeling, he adds, is a purely subjective fact, not an article of faith; it brings with it no assurance of personal immortality, but a source of religious energy seized upon by various churches and religious systems, directed by them into particular channels, and doubtless exhausted by them. One may, he thinks, rightly call oneself religious on the grounds of this oceanic feeling even if one rejects every faith and every illusion."

Freud speaks of these feelings with contempt, viewing them as a leftover from a previous stage of human evolution when we were closer to termites or wolves in a pack and had not developed the individualism that defines mankind. He writes: "I can imagine that the oceanic feeling became connected with religion later on. The 'oneness with the universe' that constitutes its ideational content sounds like a first attempt at religious consolation, as though it were another way of disclaiming the danger which the ego recognizes as threatening it from the external world."

However, Freud does not seem to realize that it is this sense of oneness and belonging in a community, of a desire to be part of a joint effort and cause greater than oneself, that laid the basis for the achievements, not just of socialism, but of all human civilization. Human beings are collective in nature, and our progress as a species has been defined by the cultivation of a collective mindset and joint effort to achieve a higher purpose.

When socialism took power across the world during the 20th century, it broke with the destructiveness of the revolutionary intelligentsia. While revolutionaries utilized the anger and releasing of impulses to take power, the Bolsheviks, the Chinese Communist Party, the Baathists and Bolivarians won the loyalty of populations by unleashing collectivism and solidarity.

Interestingly, the New Testament describes a similar feeling among the early years of the Christian Church: "They devoted themselves to the apostles' teaching and to fellowship, to the breaking of bread and to prayer. Everyone was filled with awe at the many wonders and signs performed by the apostles. All the believers were together and had everything in common. They sold property and possessions to give to anyone who had need. Every day they continued to meet together in the temple courts. They broke bread in their homes and ate together with glad and sincere hearts, praising God and enjoying the favor of all the people. And the Lord added to their number daily those who were being saved." (Acts 4: 42-47)

Zbiegnew Brzezinski & Susan Sontag

The man who probably had the greatest responsibility for the victory of the United States in the Cold War, aside from Henry Kissinger, was Zbigniew Brzezinski. He was a Polish born anti-communist who hated Russians on an ethnic level, based on hundreds of years of tension between Poland and Russia. Brzezinski studied first in Montreal and then at Harvard University, always focusing on how to roll back the influence of the Soviet Union.

Brzezinski emphasized the concept of "peaceful engagement" with the socialist countries of Eastern Europe. He urged the US government to back away from hardline, doctrinaire anti-communism, and to instead focus on manipulating Communists against each other. He became a principal strategist in the Cold War, advising US Presidents such as Kennedy, Johnson, and Reagan. Jimmy Carter called himself a "student of Zbigniew Brzezinski."

Brzezinski worked intensely with the Rockefeller's Trilateral Commission to develop a new strategy for defeating Communism in the aftermath of the defeat of the United States in the Vietnam War. He was appointed to be Jimmy Carter's National Security Advisor. Ronald Reagan awarded him the Presidential Medal of Freedom.

During the Vietnam War, many young leftists had begun to identify with the peasants of Vietnam fighting the foreign occupiers. The USA was viewed as an authoritarian force of tanks and planes, while the Vietnamese National

Liberation Front was impoverished farmers fighting in the jungles to defend their villages. Brzezinski deduced that it was necessary to hijack these sentiments that Vietnamese Communists had tapped into with their global public relations campaign opposing the presence of US troops. The idea was to set up "The Afghan Trap" to give the Soviet Union "their own Vietnam war."

In an interview with the French newspaper *Le Nouvel Observateur* he explained his thinking:

> Q: Despite this risk, you were an advocate of this covert action. But perhaps you yourself desired this Soviet entry into the war and looked for a way to provoke it?
>
> B: It wasn't quite like that. *We didn't push the Russians to intervene, but we knowingly increased the probability that they would.*
>
> Q: When the Soviets justified their intervention by asserting that they intended to fight against secret US involvement in Afghanistan, nobody believed them. However, there was an element of truth in this. You don't regret any of this today?
>
> B: Regret what? That secret operation was an excellent idea. It had the effect of *drawing the Russians into the Afghan trap* and you want me to regret it? The day that the Soviets officially crossed the border, *I wrote to President Carter, essentially: "We now have the opportunity of giving to the USSR its Vietnam war."* Indeed, for almost 10 years, Moscow had to carry on a war that was unsustainable for the regime, a conflict that brought about the demoralization and finally the breakup of the Soviet empire.
>
> Q: And neither do you regret having supported Islamic fundamentalism, which has given arms and

advice to future terrorists?

B: What is more important in world history? The Taliban or the collapse of the Soviet empire? Some agitated Moslems or the liberation of Central Europe and the end of the cold war?

CBS News was caught airing staged battle footage to make the Islamic extremists fighting the Soviet Union, led by a young Osama Bin Laden, look like romantic freedom fighters. The fake footage was exposed by the *Columbia School of Journalism Review* and the *New York Post*.

In 1989, the Associated Press confirmed the reports: "Most of the footage was shot by cameraman Mike Hoover, who allegedly staged scenes of guerrilla sabotage and made a Chinese-built Pakistani jet on a training run appear to be a Soviet plane bombing Afghan villages."

The 1987 James Bond film *The Living Daylights* was dedicated to the "brave mujahideen fighters of Afghanistan."

By appealing to the leftist aesthetics with slick propaganda, the western imperialists could defeat the Communists. Covert manipulation of leftist politics, which began with the Congress for Cultural Freedom program, escalated.

Zbigniew Brzezinski famously coined the term "Eurocommunists" in reference to the fact that in 1978, the French, Italian, and Spanish Communist Parties denounced the Soviet Union's foreign policy, echoing the very allegations against the USSR made by the US State Department. This had been the result of decades of covert manipulation. Academics had a great deal of influence within the European Communist Parties. They received grant money from CIA-linked foundations and were carefully "nudged" to emphasize social liberalism and move in an "Anti-Stalinist" direction. The Frankfurt School, covertly supported by the

CIA from as early as the 1950s, emphasized the need to focus on intellectuals, not the working class, and combined Freudian psychoanalysis with Marxism, focusing on cultural criticism.

The writings of Antonio Gramsci, an Italian Communist who wrote coded notebooks from within a fascist prison, were pushed to front while the key ideological texts of Marx and Lenin were ignored. The idea that the Soviet Union was made up of "Red Fascists" and "Totalitarians" who had betrayed the ideals of "workers democracy" and "permanent revolution" was covertly financed and pushed into leftist circles. Figures associated with the Congress for Cultural Freedom and *Partisan Review* became iconic voices of a "new left" that viewed working people as a mob of inferior rabble who threatened the independence of the intellectuals.

Susan Sontag declared in an essay called *Fascinating Fascism* written for the *New York Times Review of Books*, that many aspects of the USSR and the Eastern Bloc were somehow "fascist." She wrote: "Fascism - also stands for an ideal or rather ideals that are persistent today under the other banners: ideal of life as art, the cult of beauty, the fetishism of courage, the dissolution of alienation in the ecstatic feelings of community… the family of man…"extravagant effort, and the endurance of pain… the massing of groups of people; the turning of people into things; the multiplication and replication of things and grouping of people/things around an all-powerful hypnotic leader-figure or force. The fascist dramaturgy centers on the orgiastic transactions between mighty forces and their puppets… mass athletic demonstration, a choreographed display of bodies are a valued activity in all totalitarian countries; and the art of the gymnast, so popular now in Eastern Europe, also evokes recurrent features of fascist aesthetics; the holding in or confining of force; military precision."

In essence, Sontag argued that because the Marxist-Leninist governments mobilized their populations and unleashed a spirit of selflessness and community, they were inherently "fascist." To Sontag, whose career began with the CIA-backed *Partisan Review*, leftist politics was simply about unleashing impulses and protecting the individuality of intellectuals.

When Brzezinski helped to stage an uprising among dock workers in his homeland of Poland against the Marxist-Leninist government, many in the confused American leftist movement supported the anti-communist protests. Aside from a few hardliners such as the Communist Party USA or the Workers World Party (labelled "Stalinists" and "Tankies" by detractors), the western left embraced what was later proven to be a CIA operation intended to destabilize socialism in Poland.

At a New York City rally of Trotskyites, hippies, anarchists, and others leftists who backed the "Solidarity" movement in Poland, Susan Sontag proclaimed: "Communism is Fascism—successful Fascism, if you will. What we have called Fascism is, rather, the form of tyranny that can be overthrown—that has, largely, failed. I repeat: Not only is Fascism (and overt military rule) the probable destiny of all Communist societies—especially when their populations are moved to revolt—but Communism is in itself a variant, the most successful variant, of Fascism. Fascism with a human face."

The entire nature of left-wing politics had been changed, and remains completely distorted right up to today. It is this distortion that made the rise of Kamala Harris possible.

A Crude Freudian Manipulation

Across Eastern Europe, in China, and in many other places, the socialist governments were represented on US television as Tanks; faceless, cruel, metallic machines. Meanwhile, the US aligned dissidents were portrayed as "free thinkers," "intellectuals," and "idealists." The Marxist-Leninist regimes were portrayed as militarists crushing peace-loving hippies and artists who wanted freedom.

But underneath the New Left's rejection of class struggle, economic analysis, and embracing of "freedom" as ideal was a contempt and fear of common people. Hannah Arendt, one of the definitive New Left thinkers on Totalitarianism, wrote a piece entitled *Eichmann in Jerusalem: A Report on the Banality of Evil.* The piece focuses on Adolf Eichmann, the Nazi war criminal abducted by Mossad and executed in Jerusalem for his crimes against Jews during the holocaust. Arendt's text goes to great lengths to describe how much of a typical human being Eichmann was. The text is widely read to be a warning against conformity and "just following orders."

However, another implication is beneath Arendt's contempt for Eichmann as a "joiner" who had been part of the YMCA before joining the Nazi party. The implication is that deep down ordinary people, the working class, are all potential Nazis. The implication is that every barrier must be erected to restrain and control the ignorant rabble, to protect the enlightened few. The implication is also that those who would rally the masses to fight for their interests, against the elite and the wealthy ruling class, are inherently dangerous, even if their organizing takes place on the basis of a revolutionary, progressive platform.

In the minds that make up the entity which is rightly called "The Synthetic Left," the broad masses of people must be controlled and restrained. Social engineering, deceptive propaganda, a surveillance apparatus and police state all are necessary to make sure they never begin to assert their wishes.

Prior to the Second World War, socialism and communism in the United States were considered to be populist movements. They fought for working people against the ruling elite. They built solidarity between different races and nationalities with slogans like "Black and White, Unite and Fight!" They built unemployment councils and labor unions to win economic justice, waging a class struggle on behalf of the working class majority against the exploiting capitalist elite.

Sigmund Freud, beloved by the Frankfurt School who somehow combined the worldview of an anti-communist with Marxism, was quite outspoken in his contempt for ordinary people and the morals by which they live. Freud's text *Civilization and Its Discontents* goes as far as to mock the golden rule of Christianity: "Love your neighbor as yourself."

Freud writes: "Why should we do it? What good will it do us? But, above all, how shall we achieve it? How can it be possible? My love is something valuable to me which I ought not to throw away without reflection. It imposes duties on me for whose fulfillment I must be ready to make sacrifices."

Freud writes that much of the mental illness of the world is rooted in guilt around natural feelings of selfishness and aggression which cannot be overcome. He writes: "I remember my own defensive attitude when the idea of an instinct of destruction first emerged in psychoanalytic literature, and how long it took before I became receptive to it… For little children do not like it when there is talk of an inborn human inclination to badness, to aggressiveness and destruction, and so to cruelty as well… The commandment 'love thy neighbor as thy self' is the strongest defense against human aggressiveness and an excellent example of the unpsychological proceedings of the cultural superego. The commandment is impossible to fulfill…anyone who follows such a precept in present day civilization only puts himself at a disadvantage vis-a-vis the person who disregards it."

In the absence of class solidarity and economic notions of socialism as central planning and construction, many have noted that leftism has largely degenerated to a form of *victimology*. Various forms of oppression, racism, sexism, homophobia, transphobia, mistreatment of the disabled, and body shaming, are denounced and studied in great depth. In left-wing discourse, individuals are given permission to feel that they have been victimized for this unfairness and unleash their rage. They get to satisfy their impulse toward aggression by exacting revenge for their perceived oppression.

So, how did Kamala Harris grow up among anti-racist activists, aware of the legacy of Jim Crow and injustices of the US legal system, and yet become a sadistic perpetrator of mass incarceration? Because we cannot expect her to "love her neighbor as herself" or feel empathy for her victims. The "liberation" of a woman of color who has clearly suffered great hardship and injustice in her life is enacted by lifting moral restraints and allowing her to act out her rage.

According to the logic of Frankfurt School Cultural Critics, the post-modernists, Sigmund Freud, and other pseudo-leftists who view Marxism as merely a vehicle for deconstruction, Kamala Harris' life is a beautiful thing. A person from historically marginalized groups has become empowered to unleash her rage on to the world. The myths that once held society together and restrained such behavior have been deconstructed.

The psychology of the revolutionary intelligentsia, when stripped of any scientific Marxist ideology; the mindset of angry crowds screaming around the guillotine; has become incarnated in an age where Twitter anger and "wokeness" has replaced the notion of human progress.

Kamala Harris is the logical conclusion of a long process of distorting leftist politics, and reducing it to a crude, Freudian manipulation.

3. The Geopolitical Stage

In 2017, the celebrity gossip website *Page Six* blew the whistle on what was probably intended to be a secret meeting in Long Island, New York. Emily Smith wrote: "The Democrats' "Great Freshman Hope," Sen. Kamala Harris, is heading to the Hamptons to meet with Hillary Clinton's biggest backers. The California senator is being fêted in Bridgehampton on Saturday at the home of MWWPR guru Michael Kempner, a staunch Clinton supporter who was one of her national-finance co-chairs and a led fundraiser for her 2008 bid for the presidency. He was also listed as one of the top "bundlers" for Barack Obama's 2012 re-election campaign, having raised $3 million."

The article went on to describe others who were meeting behind the prosecutor turned politician: "Guests there to greet Harris are expected to include Margo Alexander, a member of Clinton's inner circle; Dennis Mehiel, a Democratic donor who is the chairman of the Battery Park City Authority, even though he lives between a sprawling Westchester estate and an Upper East Side pad; designer Steven Gambrel and Democratic National Committee member Robert Zimmerman. Washington lobbyist Liz Robbins is also hosting a separate Hamptons lunch for Harris."

A Fight Behind Closed Doors

An article further reporting on the events described Harris' connection to another Clinton backer, the Hungarian billionaire George Soros. Writing for *The Observer*,

Michael Sainato wrote: "In 2011, Harris' former aide Lenore Anderson was hired as campaign manager for Californians for Safety and Justice, which was financed by Soros' Open Society Foundations.... since 2012 Soros had led a four-year, $16 million campaign to change California criminal policy, which Harris was deeply involved in as California attorney general. Lenore Anderson also led Vote Safe, another Soros funded organization."

With Clinton's continued attempts to test the waters for a 2020 run falling flat, Kamala Harris was the new pick of her top financial backers. Things looked good for Kamala heading toward the 2020 Democratic Primary. She was only a freshman Senator, but she was a charismatic speaker and was making a name for herself grandstanding against Trump and interrogating his allies at televised congressional hearings.

A definitive moment for Kamala's Presidential campaign came on July 31, 2019 when Hawaii Congresswoman Tulsi Gabbard used her limited time to make a short speech, exposing Harris' record as a prosecutor. This was an odd decision for Tulsi Gabbard to make. Gabbard was treated as a fringe candidate and received very limited time on the debate stage.

Why use the few moments of national airtime to single out a single top-tier rival? Keep in mind that Kamala was not even among the top two front runners. Understanding Gabbard's motivation gets to the essence of understanding the danger posed by Kamala Harris.

While serving in the House of Representatives, Tulsi Gabbard remained a member of the Army National Guard. She served a tour of duty in Iraq. Despite being a member of the military, Gabbard's campaign focused on her anti-war platform and her call to stop arming terrorists in Syria and engaging in "regime change wars." Illustrating her platform, Gabbard explained: "We have spent trillions of dollars on regime change wars in the Middle East while communities like Hawaii face a severe lack of affordable housing, aging infrastructure, the need to invest in education, health care, and so much more."

Gabbard's website describes the landmark legislation she proposed, the Stop Arming Terrorists Act (H.R. 608) that "would stop the U.S. government from using taxpayer dollars to directly or indirectly support groups who are allied with and supporting terrorist groups like ISIS and al Qaeda in their war to overthrow the Syrian government. The legislation is based on congressional action during the Iran-Contra affair to stop the CIA's illegal arming of rebels in Nicaragua. It is endorsed by Progressive Democrats of America, the U.S. Peace Council, and Veterans For Peace."

Congresswoman Tulsi Gabbard, whose Presidential campaign focused on opposing regime change wars, specifically called out Kamala Harris for her record as a prosecutor.

Gabbard's Presidential campaign was almost immediately attacked in the press, in addition to being often outright ignored. Hillary Clinton attempted to link Tulsi Gabbard to Russia, and in response Gabbard filed a defamation lawsuit. The fact that Gabbard met with Syrian President Bashar Assad, in a trip organized by the Christian-led Syrian Social Nationalist Party, was also widely criticized.

Though Gabbard's campaign was highly unsuccessful, her takedown of Kamala Harris knocked her out of the race. Tulsi's few sentences exposing Kamala and Kamala's lack of an effective rebuttal turned the tides. On the debate stage Kamala Harris could barely muster any response to Gabbard's very true exposition of her political record and obvious lack of moral compass. In a follow up conversation with Anderson Cooper after the debate on CNN, Harris was once again given an opportunity to rebut Gabbard's remarks. All she could muster was to bait Gabbard for her alleged sympathies for the Syrian government.

Following the July 31st debate, Harris began to sink in the polls. Harris' agitational style, castigating Trump with a pointed finger and invoking the racism and hardship of her childhood was certainly charming at first.

However, millions of Americans were led by Tulsi Gabbard to see Kamala Harris not simply as a person who would use her oral skills to prosecute Donald Trump, but as someone who would happily use it against their innocent fathers, brothers, sons, and daughters without remorse, in the hopes of simply advancing her career. Kamala no longer seemed bold, but rather quite frightening. The public rejected Kamala Harris at the polls. Bernie Sanders, attacked by the media for his alleged ties to Cuba, much like Karen Bass would later be attacked, did far better among the voters.

However, the selection of her as VP nominee, with Joe Biden's frail elderly condition, has her once again on the fast track to Head of State, despite the American people's better judgement.

So, why did Gabbard utilize her limited time on the debate stage to target a single candidate? Furthermore, why was a member of the Army National Guard running on an anti-war platform? This also leads us back to the opening questions, about why Harris' nomination for Vice President was so last minute, and surrounded by so much confusion.

The reality is that a fight is taking place at the top of US society, mostly behind closed doors. The fight goes on across party lines, within intelligence agencies and inside the so-called "deep state" apparatus, and within the financial business elite. Essentially, forces from many different angles are trying to hold off the destructive agenda of one very dangerous and powerful clique.

The Honduran Coup of 2009

Hillary Clinton ran the US State Department from 2009 to 2013. It is doubtful that any individual US official has ever done so much damage to the global community in such short a time. Clinton was backed by the same forces that now financially back Kamala Harris. She had a slew of staffers including Jared Cohen, Samantha Power, Anne-Marie Slaughter, and Susan Rice.

On the 28th of June, 2009, the Honduran Military toppled the elected government. Manuel Zelaya, who won the elections fair and square according to every poll and observer, was overthrown. In her book *Hard Choices,* Clinton claims he was removed due to "fears that he was preparing to circumvent the constitution and extend his term in office." This is false.

Zelaya had been in the process of taking a non-binding poll among the Honduran public about whether or not they would favor the ratification of a new constitution. In Venezuela and Bolivia, the Bolivarian governments had ratified a new constitution to move the country toward socialism. Zelaya simply wanted to see if there was a popular mandate for doing so in Honduras before proposing it to the legislators. The military, trained and armed by the US government, was determined to make sure that did not happen.

Manuel Zelaya was kidnapped at gunpoint by the military and flown out of the country in his pajamas. A military junta assumed power. The results of this coup in Honduras have been horrendous. In 2009, Honduras already had the highest homicide rate in the world due to the prevalence of drug cartels among the impoverished population. From 2008 to 2011, the murder rate increased in Honduras by 50%.

The US-backed free market regime has not only presided over extreme poverty in Honduras, but it has maintained power through political assassinations. LGBT activists in particular have been targeted by right-wing kill squads aligned with the drug gangs.

Immediately following the coup, US President Barack Obama told the press that the moves by the Honduras military had been "not legal." However, Hillary Clinton's State Department had been heavily involved in the coup long before it happened. Jake Johnstone wrote an article for *The Intercept* published on August 29, 2017, describing how top leaders of the Honduran military had been taking classes with the US Department of Defense. The coup plotters were all well connected to the US military brass and friendly with members of Congress.

While Barack Obama appears to have learned of the Honduran Coup when it occurred, Hillary Clinton had been tipped off by Hugo Llorens, US ambassador to Honduras a week before. The US State Department had then dispatched John D. Negroponte to meet with the coup plotters. Negroponte had a history of ties to political violence in Central America, going back to the Contra War in Nicaragua during the 1980s. He had also been involved with the Battalion 3-16 that had murdered 200 people in Honduras.

After the coup, as the wave of assassinations of political dissidents began, the Hillary Clinton State Department showered funds on a propaganda campaign for the new regime. "In 2012, as Honduras descended into social and political chaos in the wake of a US-sanctioned military coup, the civilian aid arm of Hillary Clinton's State Department spent over $26 million on a propaganda program aimed at encouraging anti-violence "alliances" between Honduran community groups and local police and security forces," writes Tim Shorrock for *The Nation* on April 5th, 2016. "The program, called "Honduras Convive," was designed by the US Agency for International Development (USAID) to reduce violent crimes in a country that had simultaneously become the murder capital of the world and a staging ground for one of the largest deployments of US Special Operations forces outside of the Middle East." A total of roughly $57 million in aid was provided to the Honduran government by the US State Department from 2009 to 2014.

According to the CIA World Factbook, over 12%, well over 1 in 10 Hondurans, cannot read or write. The infant mortality rate is a whopping 14.6 deaths for every thousand live births. As drug violence persists and access to running water and electricity remains unavailable to large chunks of the population, many of the thousands of refugees found at the US border are Hondurans.

The bodycount of Hillary Clinton's State Department in Honduras is most likely in the hundreds of thousands. Hillary Clinton enabled the violent overthrow of a democratically elected government, and then proceeded to throw money at a death squad regime. The 2009 coup, and the continued propping up of this regime with US military personnel and funding which she launched, and to which Obama may have at first been oblivious, has resulted in continued instability in this small country of just 9 million people south of the US border.

Malnutrition, lack of access to healthcare, lack of access to clean drinking water, drug gang violence, and political repression have taken a tremendous humanitarian toll. The violence has spilled over into Mexico and other parts of the region. It has contributed to the overall decline of living standards in the region.

The Arab Spring

The Arab Spring events of 2011 were not spontaneous. They were said to begin when Tunisian fruit seller Mohamed Bouazizi lit himself on fire in December of 2010. However, suicides, even theatrical ones, often go unnoticed. In Muslim countries the press makes a bigger point of not highlighting suicides for religious reasons.

The reason that Bouazizi's recorded self-immolation sparked a series of events was not simply because it happened, but because it went viral. Videos of the flames and the small local uprisings shot across facebook and twitter. Al-Jazeera, the TV network owned by the US-backed autocracy in Qatar, highlighted the events as well.

In 2016, it was confirmed what had long been suspected. The *Wall Street Journal* reported: "Facebook Inc. exerts more editorial control than it previously disclosed over the "trending" news feature on the social network, newly posted documents show." News stories do not "go viral" randomly based on how many clicks and likes they get. Rather, a select group of "News Curators" who are not immune from political bias, carefully manipulate the algorithms, deciding what stories show up on individual newsfeeds. (*Wall Street Journal*, May 12, 2016)

In her State Department, Hillary Clinton had selected Jared Andrew Cohen to direct social media operations. Cohen is a Rhodes Scholar and member of the Council on Foreign Relations. He is currently the CEO of Jigsaw, the corporation previously known as Google Ideas. Long before Clinton had worked at the State Department, Jared Cohen had participated in Clinton's "Policy Planning Staff" from 2006 to 2010.

Jared Andrew Cohen contacted Twitter on behalf of the US State Department, pushing them to take actions that would benefit anti-government protesters in Iran. The Obama administration was furious about this, but Hillary Clinton protected him.

In 2009, Jared Cohen contacted Twitter, asking them to help facilitate protests against the Iranian government in the hopes of destabilizing the government and overthrowing the Ayatollahs. In doing so, he went directly against the wishes and policies of the White House.

An article published in *The New Yorker* on April 25, 2011, cites an unnamed official reporting that Cohen "almost lost his job over it. If it had been up to the White House, they would have fired him." Cohen took the move in direct disobedience to Obama, but in full obedience to Hillary Clinton. The article states: "Clinton did not betray any disagreement with the President over Iran policy, but in an interview with me she cited Cohen's action with pride."

Anne-Marie Slaughter, an academic who was essential in the Hillary Clinton State Department, loves the fact that Clinton took office intent on spreading unrest across the planet: "Secretary Clinton can push the agenda she pushes because she is tough and people know she is tough." Anne-Marie Slaughter is heavily influenced by Zbigniew Brzezinski. She speaks of a new form of governance through global networks. Her books with titles such as *A New World Order* and *The Chessboard and The Web* talk of destabilizing and overthrowing governments, paving the way for "open governments, open societies, and an open international system."

The Middle East was a ticking time bomb in 2010. Mass unemployment in the urban centers due to the financial crisis, and massive drought affecting the rural population all saw unrest on the horizon. The Hillary Clinton State Department decided to take a match to the tinderbox. With memories of the 1979 revolution in Iran or the rise of Baathist Arab Socialism in their minds, fearing uncontrolled unrest and the rise of anti-imperialist forces, the

Hillary Clinton state department pre-empted any explosion or organic resistance with a controlled demolition.

The fact that America's first African-American President, a man with a Muslim middle name who had attended an Islamic elementary school, sat at the Presidency, was key in making the magic happen. Rather than pouring into the streets to chant "Death to America," the confused crowds could be covertly directed by social media and Qatari state media. The Muslim Brotherhood, a longtime soft power proxy of US power in Egypt, Syria, and other countries throughout the region would be the most influential force in manipulating events. The Muslim Brotherhood had been utilized by the CIA to work against Arab Socialist leader Gamal Abdul Nasser in Egypt during the 1950s. In the 1980s, leaders of the Muslim Brotherhood had staged a violent uprising against the Syrian Arab Republic, supported by the United States in their efforts to topple Baathist Arab Socialism. Israel had even covertly supported the Muslim Brotherhood in the 1980s in order to divide Palestinian resistance. A *Wall Street Journal* article from January 24th, 2009 quotes Avner Cohen, a former religious affairs official in Israel, as saying: "Hamas, to my great regret, is Israel's creation." Avner has been very public about the fact that he and other Israeli officials covertly supported the Muslim Brotherhood in Palestine in its efforts to attack Marxist Palestinian organizations like the Popular Front for the Liberation of Palestine. Eventually, from the Muslim Brotherhood in Palestine emerged Hamas.

The Muslim Brotherhood significantly gained from the Arab Spring. In Egypt, Mohamed Morsi was elected President. In Tunisia, the Muslim Brotherhood gained a huge increase in political influence. Of course, amid such events, all kinds of forces poured into the streets. Iran hailed an "Islamic Awakening" hoping to push the protesters toward Shia Islam and its tradition of resistance to oppression. Communists also joined the protests in Egypt and elsewhere. However, the news curators of social media and the producers of CNN arranged for the world to look the other way as Saudi Arabia invaded Bahrain to prop up the autocratic monarchy and slaughter the Shia majority, who protested for their human rights. The Yemeni people's revolutionary uprisings, which set the stage for the eventual seizure of power by Ansarullah and the Revolutionary Committee in 2015, was also ignored.

Amid the chaos, Hillary Clinton's State Department worked to specifically target two anti-imperialist, socialist states. The first target was Libya. Until 2011, Libya had the highest life expectancy on the entire African continent. The country had universal housing and literacy. Gaddafi had constructed the Great Man Made River, the largest irrigation system in the world. Libya was leading talks of creating an independent African currency.

In order to topple the most prosperous government in Africa, the US State Department facilitated a flow of religious fanatics into Libya. Among them was Salman Ramadan Abedi, who would return to his home country of Britain and bomb the Manchester Arena, killing 23 people.

What Hillary Clinton and her allies claimed was a glorious revolution was a bloodbath of religious fanaticism and racism. The *New York Times* was forced to reveal the fact that anti-Gaddafi Libyans were lynching dark skinned guest workers with a headline from Sept. 5th, 2011 reading "Libyans turn wrath on dark-skinned migrants." As social media rallied instability in Libya, social media conveniently agitated the public with slogans like "Gaddaffi is killing us with his Africans."

Clinton protege Susan Rice told the press that Gaddaffi was distributing Viagra in order to encourage his soldiers to engage in mass rape. Amnesty International later debunked this claim.

The results of overthrowing the Islamic socialist government of Libya have been disastrous. Conditions have become so bad in Libya since it has joined Anne-Marie Slaughter's "open international system" that people are packing into boats by the thousands to flee. Since 2013, over 700,000 Libyans have crossed the Mediterranean into Europe on boats. Hundreds have died in numerous instances where these ships have sunk.

In 2017, the world was shocked to discover the existence of open air slave markets in Libyan cities. Much of the country remains without electricity. Instability persists as different factions battle for power. Jihadist groups had significantly increased their presence in the region, and much of the instability in Mali and other countries has been linked to the toppling of the Libyan government.

Video surfaced of Hillary Clinton being informed about the death of the socialist leader who raised millions from poverty in Libya. Much like the way Kamala Harris cackled with delight about imprisoning the parents of low income children, Clinton giggles and proclaims "We came. We saw. He died."

The Syrian Arab Republic, a hold-out of Baathist Arab Socialism, was also targeted. The life expectancy in Syria increased by 17 years from 1970 to 2009 due the huge efforts of the socialist government to provide medical care and train doctors. Infant mortality dropped dramatically from 132 deaths per 1,000 live births to only 17.9 during the period, according to the Avicenna Journal of Medicine.

The U.S. Library of Congress Country Study of Syria, published in 1987, described huge achievements in the field of education conducted by the Baath socialist state. During the 1980s, for the first time in Syria's history, the country achieved "full primary school enrollment of males." At the time the study was published, 85 percent of females also enrolled in primary school. In 1981, 42 percent of Syria's adult population was illiterate, but by 1991 illiteracy had been wiped out.

The Soviet Union had cooperated with the Syrian government to engage in big construction projects including the Taqba Dam on the Euphrates River, which enabled irrigation of the countryside and provided hydroelectric power to the population. In more recent decades, China had increased its cooperation with the Baath Socialists. In 2007, the Jamestown Foundation reported that China had invested "hundreds of millions of dollars" in Syria in efforts to "modernize the country's aging oil and gas infrastructure."

But Hillary Clinton and her wrecking crew moved in to destroy it. The Syrian Arab Republic had already been labelled as a "state sponsor of terrorism" due to its arming of the Palestinians. The fact that it had turned down the proposal to build an oil pipeline with the US-aligned autocracies of Qatar and Saudi Arabia, but instead was working to build one with the Islamic Republic of Iran, was also most likely a factor driving the destruction of a previously peaceful Arab country.

The Syrian government attempted to accommodate the concerns of the protesters who took to the streets in 2011, ratifying a new constitution. Because many of the protesters were Sunni Muslims, influenced by the Muslim Brotherhood and Saudi Arabia to oppose Bashar Assad as a "Shia apostate" for his Alawite religious background, the new constitution specifically honored Sunni Islam. Assad began praying in Sunni mosques and engaging in other activities that are not done by Alawites in order to show solidarity with the Sunni majority.

The USA began arming and training extremists to tear down the Syrian Arab Republic almost immediately after the 2011 "Arab Spring" protests. In 2013, the BBC published a "guide to Syrian rebels." Listed among them was not only the infamous "Islamic State" organization, but also the Nusra Front, previously known as Al-Qaida in Syria. Other organizations with names like the "Islamic Front," the "Islamic Liberation Front," and the "Ahfad al-Rasoul Brigades" were also listed. While US media, Al-Jazeera, Twitter, and Facebook dazzled western audiences with a story of "revolutionaries" fighting for "human rights" against a dictator, the reality is that the anti-Assad coalition was primarily concerned about ending religious freedom and establishing a Saudi style Wahabbi autocracy.

Early on in the fighting, UN official Carla Del Ponte confirmed that the US-backed terrorists in Syria were utilizing chemical weapons in their fight against the government. Child soldiers made up a significant percentage of the anti-government fighting force. Homeless children and orphans throughout the region were being shipped to Syria, indoctrinated into the Saudi brand of Islamic extremism, and sent to die in the fight to overthrow Baathist Arab Socialism.

The humanitarian cost of the conflict in Syria, which the Hillary Clinton State Department engineered, has been well over 500,000 lives. Millions of Syrians have become refugees. The Syrian government remains intact, despite relentless efforts to overthrow it.

Russia and Iran have offered significant support to the Syrian government. Hezbollah fighters from Lebanon were decisive in defeating the ISIS terrorists who emerged from within the US-backed anti-Assad coalition. Qassem Soleimani, who Donald Trump assassinated with a drone on January 3, 2020, was key in fighting to protect Christians and religious minorities from US-backed fanatics in Syria as a leader of the Islamic Revolutionary Guard Corps of Iran.

Conflict Within The Deep State
In April of 2016, when asked about his biggest regret about his presidency in a FOX News interview, Barack Obama said: "probably failing to plan for the day after what I think was the right thing to do in intervening in Libya." Later in the interview Obama stated that the intervention "did not work." Furthermore, in May of 2017, Obama described his decision not to attack Syria with cruise missiles in 2013 as his "most courageous decision" as President.

What is interesting about both of these moments is that Hillary Clinton and her State Department were heavily involved. In 2011, Hillary Clinton and Samantha Power pushed very hard for Obama to intervene in Libya. Obama did so, and regrets the results and the manner of the intervention. In 2013, Hillary Clinton also pushed for Obama to directly attack the Syrian Arab Republic in response to allegations about chemical weapons. Obama did not do so, and considered this a great moment. This reveals what was also hinted at when Obama attempted to fire Jared Cohen over his meddling in Iran via twitter. The Obama administration was at odds with the Hillary Clinton State Department.

Barack Obama replaced Hillary Clinton with John Kerry as Secretary of State in his second term. John Kerry focused not on spreading revolution and destabilizing countries, but rather on establishing diplomatic relations with Cuba and negotiating the Iran Nuclear Deal. Kerry's State Department seemed not to clash with the White House to any significant degree.

But the Obama White House was not the only faction within the US government apparatus that seemed to realize how dangerous the actions of Hillary Clinton's State Department really were. Amid the 2013 crisis, when it appeared Obama was on the brink of launching cruise missiles against the Syrian government, many rank and file soldiers expressed disgust on social media.

On Sept. 1, 2013, mainstream outlet *Business Insider* observed: "As the march to limited military intervention in Syria moves forward, some troops are making their views known, albeit anonymously on social media. Photos of service members have apparently popped up on Reddit, seemingly in protest of Syrian intervention… The basic argument is that the line between moderate rebel factions and Al-Qaeda-affiliated ones are somewhat murky in the two-year-old civil war, so the U.S. should stay away."

Indeed, many within the US intelligence agencies, military brass, and state department learn to speak and read Arabic in order to do their jobs. It is likely that many of those who are motivated by a desire to defeat terrorism and protect American civilians from another 9/11 were horrified to discover that the US government was actively arming the entities that would eventually establish an Islamic State. In Syria, just like Afghanistan during the 1980s or in Libya during the 2011 "revolution," the US government was not opposing the terrorists. The USA was helping and arming the terrorists in the hopes of destabilizing a socialist state.

So, understanding that many within the Pentagon realized the harsh realities of what was done by the Hillary Clinton State Department, it should not be surprising that an Army National Guard soldier became the primary Congressional voice in opposition to destabilizing Syria by arming terrorists. Tulsi Gabbard represents a whole layer of people within the Pentagon who are disillusioned with the "humanitarian intervention" "regime change" foreign policy of the United States. Pentagon figures like retired Lt. General Michael Flynn, who went on to briefly serve as National Security Advisor to Donald Trump, made similar statements.

It should not be surprising that during her Presidential Campaign, Gabbard used her limited time to verbally take down the newly selected candidate of the faction behind Hillary Clinton's State Department. The specific group of wealthy donors that Kamala Harris met with in the Hamptons, who had put their money behind Hillary Clinton, made a group decision to pick Kamala Harris as their new "great hope" in 2017.

Her personality profile and career history seemed to match what they were looking for. The forces that seek to create an "open society" at the cost of unlimited human lives have lined up behind Kamala Harris. The utopian bloodlust of the revolutionary intelligentsia has been hijacked to serve imperialism. The "permanent revolution" the Soviet people rejected is now being taken up by western intelligence agencies. It is no longer intended to empower the proletariat, but to unleash the impulses of millions and tear apart the "authoritarianism" of civilization which restrains capitalist greed.

It shouldn't be surprising that Joe Biden, who sided with the White House against Clinton's State Department, would be reluctant to add Kamala Harris to the 2020 ticket. It is not surprising that he would delay the decision as long as possible, and scour the party for any possible alternative.

It fits this narrative, that as Karen Bass appeared from nowhere in the eyes of the media as suddenly being a potential VP pick, a dossier of information about her alleged ties to the Cuban government suddenly found its way to the front pages. Who keeps track of Cuba's contacts in the United States and monitors who travels to the socialist island? Who compiled such information on Karen Bass, and kept it on file in case she was ever to gain significant traction?

Many people behind the scenes know who is behind Kamala Harris. They know how many millions of lives were needlessly destroyed by the Hillary Clinton State Department. They know how terrorist groups expanded, a refugee crisis was created, and global instability persists long after the demented experiment with social media and "revolution" concluded in 2013.

The fact that Trump made statements on the campaign trail about how "Hillary Clinton literally created ISIS" was no accident. The facts described in this text may not appear on CNN, but they are well known to numerous people within many layers of what have now been labelled "The Deep State."

Somehow, Kamala Harris overcame her many opponents. Her faction was able to maneuver its way to secure her position as Vice President, despite Biden's reluctance and the voters' lack of interest in this supposed "rock star" freshman Senator.

When Kamala Harris accepted the nomination on August 19th at the Democratic National Convention, her remarks and the video that preceded them were predictable. Kamala mentioned her father in passing, but eulogized her mother in glowing terms.

When talking about her accomplishments as a prosecutor, Kamala Harris declared: "I've fought for children, and survivors of sexual assault. I've fought against transnational gangs. I took on the biggest banks, and helped take down one of the biggest for-profit colleges. I know a predator when I see one." The sentence "I know a predator when I see one" was followed by an awkward pause.

Meanwhile, after Harris was announced, many media outlets and Trump supporters had been highlighting the fact that on April 2, 2019, Kamala Harris stated she believed four of the women who accused Joe Biden of sexual assault. Harris had said, "I believe them, and I respect them being able to tell their story and having the courage to do it." No retraction of her statement was ever given.

The line from Kamala's acceptance speech seemed to be an affirmation that her assessment of Joe Biden had been correct. If indeed she "knows a predator" when she sees one, she would have been correct in believing his accusers. Most interpreted the comment as merely a reference to the widespread allegations that Donald Trump sexually assaulted women, but such a statement at the Democratic National Convention would not be coded or followed by an awkward pause.

One wonders what heated exchanges took place behind closed doors in the lead-up to Joe Biden's announcement that Kamala was his VP pick. The fact that Kamala's name appeared separate from the VP nominee on the Democratic Convention Speakers schedule, published just shortly before the announcement, or that Kamala's Twitter account "unfollowed" Joe Biden just a few hours before, is also very telling.

It seems Joe Biden did not want to nominate the woman who invoked his ties to segregationists, and was backed by the same forces that spawned the Hillary Clinton State Department, an entity which he and Obama tried to contain. Something changed Joe Biden's mind right before finally announcing his selected running-mate. The decision came a full ten days after the deadline Biden had given himself.

The Specter of Populism

Karl Marx began the Communist Manifesto in 1848 with the catchy line, "A specter is haunting Europe. It is the specter of communism!" It has been noted too that the first English translation hilariously began with the words, "A frightful hobgoblin is haunting Europe."

However, what was Marx alluding to with his opening line? He was alluding to the fact that despite the fact that no real organized revolutionary movement of the proletariat existed, the atmosphere was charged with the realization that such a force was imminent. It was only a matter of time before the factory workers who were being driven to work harder and harder for lower and lower pay, organized themselves not simply to fight for better conditions, but to seize control of the state and the major commanding heights of economic power. Long before Marx had uttered the words "dictatorship of the proletariat" the capitalists, independent observers, and many others had assumed it was only a matter of time before a movement demanding such a thing existed. The "specter" was indeed haunting Europe, and the Communist Manifesto was written because: "It is high time that Communists should openly, in the face of the whole world, publish their views, their aims, their tendencies, and meet this nursery tale of the Spectre of Communism with a manifesto of the party itself."

A similar situation existed in the aftermath of the 2008-2009 financial crisis. Headlines such as "We're all socialists now" and talk of Karl Marx came from the bourgeoisie itself. They understood that the circumstances would most likely give rise to a revived opposition to the profit-based economic system and interest in Marxism would grow. Before such sentiments emerged from the masses, it seemed, warnings of it were pouring out of the pages of the *New York Times*.

There has certainly been an expansion of nominally socialist groups and left-wing activism in the United States since 2008. Occupy Wall Street, Black Lives Matter, and the wave of support for Bernie Sanders among young liberals certainly represents a political shift. However, this political shift was weakened by the very corruption of leftist politics that gave birth to Kamala Harris.

Decades and decades of covert funding and manipulation has significantly exaggerated the tendencies of the revolutionary intelligentsia. Efforts that began as an attempt to create a gap between western radicals and existing socialism have completely reinvented the definition of Marxism. The absence of class struggle politics and the obsession with individualism and identity politics rendered the left quite ineffective in the aftermath of the 2008 financial crisis.

Anti-populism, identity politics, oppression theory, and an obsession with the unleashing of sexual impulses and rage has rendered the socialist movement far more than ineffective. Instead of being a vehicle for the working class to seize power and reinvent society, the various manifestations of leftism that currently exist, be they social-democracy, Anarchism, Trotskyism, or whatnot, have become a vehicle for destabilizing anti-imperialist states. They more effectively secure the rule of the big corporations across the planet.

Wherever Wall Street is looking to topple an anti-imperialist state, the protests against it cheered by US media inevitably involve teenagers in Che Guevara T-shirts and Guy Fox masks. The forces of free market capitalism can always depend on a movement that has been reduced to an expression of adolescent rebellion being manipulated in their service.

The internet is filled with young, confused radicals pouring out hatred against their parents, their teachers, and various public figures for allegedly being "racist", "sexist", or "transphobic." New forms of oppression to be tweeted against, such as "fatphobia" and "smokerphobia" seem to be invented each day. The latest social crime of some celebrity seems to be constantly trending. To them China, the Soviet Union, Venezuela, and other anti-imperialist and socialist states are all "fascist." The only supposed revolutionary movement in the world they can bring themselves to support is the Kurdish YPG, which is also being openly supported by the CIA.

In the absence of the populistic rhetoric that made William Z. Foster, Eugene Debs, Elizabeth Gurly Flynn, and Huey Newton into effective mass organizers, the right-wing has hijacked the populist ethos. Many wrote of Trump transforming the Republican Party into a "party of the working class." Trump's inaugural address opened with these interesting few paragraphs:

> *For too long, a small group in our nation's Capitol has reaped the rewards of government while the people have borne the cost.*

Washington flourished – but the people did not share in its wealth.

Politicians prospered – but the jobs left, and the factories closed.

The establishment protected itself, but not the citizens of our country.

Their victories have not been your victories; their triumphs have not been your triumphs; and while they celebrated in our nation's Capitol, there was little to celebrate for struggling families all across our land.

That all changes – starting right here, and right now, because this moment is your moment: it belongs to you.

The Snake

However, the Trump administration has acted completely contrary to the sentiments behind these words. Rather than fighting for those deprived of wealth in this country, Trump has lifted taxes and regulations on the most wealthy. Rather than ending wars, he has escalated international tensions, murdered a top Iranian general, bombed Syria as Obama refused to do, and attempted to stage a violent military coup in Venezuela.

Rather than address the concerns about liberty being restricted, the White House has escalated the police state. Federal officers have been sent to Portland to grab protesters off of the street. At a moment when police brutality and the devaluing of African-American life has been widely recognized, Trump has positioned himself as a defender of the police. He has argued that the police are too restrained in their violence against protesters, and favors an escalation of brutality and repression.

Trump takes every opportunity to accuse his detractors of being communists and defends the system which puts profits over people as being inherently American. Trump often presents himself as being rich, tough, and unconcerned about the needs of other people.

The problematic aspects of Kamala Harris' psyche, her desire to harm others and indifference to the results of her actions, manifests itself in Trump most certainly. However, Trump expresses his destructive impulses in a different way. In much of Trump's rhetoric one finds a disturbing theme of celebrating the dark phenomenon often described as "man's inhumanity to man," or in other cases merely as a selfish indifference to the suffering of others.

On the campaign trail in 2016, as Trump demonized immigrant workers, he recited the lyrics to 1960s soul musician Oscar Brown Jr.'s song "The Snake." The song was made popular by Al Wilson. The lyrics told of a woman who mistakenly takes compassion on an injured snake, and after taking it home and caring for it, is bitten by it. The lyrics recited by Trump go as follows:

On her way to work one morning
Down the path alongside the lake
A tender-hearted woman saw a poor half-frozen snake
His pretty colored skin had been all frosted with the dew
"Oh well," she cried, "I'll take you in and I'll take care of
  you"
"Take me in oh tender woman
Take me in, for heaven's sake
Take me in oh tender woman," sighed the snake
She wrapped him up all cozy in a curvature of silk
And then laid him by the fireside with some honey and
  some milk
Now she hurried home from work that night as soon as she
  arrived
She found that pretty snake she'd taken in had been revived

> "Take me in, oh tender woman
> Take me in, for heaven's sake
> Take me in oh tender woman," sighed the snake
> Now she clutched him to her bosom, "You're so beautiful," she cried
> "But if I hadn't brought you in by now you might have died"
> Now she stroked his pretty skin and then she kissed and held him tight
> But instead of saying thanks, that snake gave her a vicious bite
> "Take me in, oh tender woman
> Take me in, for heaven's sake
> Take me in oh tender woman," sighed the snake
> "I saved you," cried that woman
> "And you've bit me even, why?
> You know your bite is poisonous and now I'm going to die"
> "Oh shut up, silly woman," said the reptile with a grin
> "You knew damn well I was a snake before you took me in

The implication of Trump's recitation of "The Snake" are that immigrant workers pose a danger and that our compassion for them is naive and potentially self destructive. However, the implications of the poem go further. The poem implies that compassion itself is foolish and weak. Humans should not be "suckers" who want to help the downtrodden, but instead should simply pursue their own self-interest.

Not surprisingly, many of Trump's supporters have studied the writings of the objectivist Ayn Rand, who spoke of capitalism as an "unknown ideal" of a world without a government where all human solidarity has been broken down and "the virtue of selfishness" prevails. Many of his supporters see Trump not as a defender of the common people, but as a non-conforming, selfish billionaire much like Ayn Rand's fictional John Galt. Trump most likely sees himself as a powerful *ubermenschen*, not concerned about the impact of his actions on inferior, lesser beings.

Education For Death

There is a fascistic edge to this kind of "libertarian" rhetoric, though it flows directly from the western liberal ideal that celebrates individualism above all else. One is forced to think of a depiction of the education of children in Nazi Germany widely circulated during the Second World War, in the cartoon short film entitled *Education For Death* from Walt Disney Productions. The 11-minute film created in 1943 features one scene in which a Nazi schoolteacher tells a class of students about a wolf chasing down and devouring a rabbit.

"Now let's see what they will learn from this little lesson?"asks the narrator. A child meekly answers in German, with the teacher giving an angry response. The narrator continues, explaining why the child's response was met with hostility: "He said the poor rabbit. Is he out of his mind? What would the Fuhrer think of such an answer? What would Herr Goring think? And Herr Goebbels?"

"Now then, who can give the correct answer?" The teacher continues, turning to the rest of the students. One boy immediately speaks up, proclaiming "The world belongs to the strong!" "And to the brutal!" Another chimes in. "The rabbit is a coward and deserves to die. I spit on the rabbit," another student adds.

The teacher then turns to the original child who first spoke with empathy for the devoured creature. Suddenly, the child speaks up, now learning to kill the empathy and basic human instincts of compassion within him, stuttering out the party line. The narrator explains: "He hates the rabbit! There's no room for weaklings. Little Hans is learning fast. My, how he hates that rabbit!"

"Hans has come around to the correct Nazi way of thinking!" The teacher announces. The narrator continues: "Yes, this lesson is the basis for the Nazi creed. Germany will likewise destroy all weak and cowardly nations." The class of students begin giving the Nazi salute to their teacher, chanting "Seig Heil! Seig Heil!"

While the modern right-wing attempts to claim that Nazism is a left-wing ideology and laughs off the accusations of fascism hurled at them, they cannot avoid this simple moral question. Fascism is based on the concept of might makes right, and seeks to eliminate the human side of human beings, reducing them to the mentality of predatory beasts.

In his review of Ayn Rand's novel *Atlas Shrugged,* even the anti-communist McCarthyist stool pigeon Whittaker Chambers could not conceal his revulsion. Writing for *National Review*, Chambers described Ayn Rand's text this way: "From almost any page of *Atlas Shrugged* a voice can be heard from painful necessity, commanding: "To the gas chamber—go!"

While the Nazis invoked a notion of solidarity and brotherhood among Germans, and referred to themselves as "National Socialists," like Benito Mussolini in Italy, they were covertly backed by British intelligence in their struggle for power against the Communist revolutionaries. Social darwinism, eugenics, survival of the fittest, might makes right, and other such concepts were developed and promoted to justify the economic theories of Adam Smith. Nazi ideology was an incarnation of British imperial ideals, not the rich history of German culture.

Free market capitalism, most especially in its monopoly stage of imperialism, identified by Vladimir Lenin in his groundbreaking text *Imperialism: The Highest Stage of Capitalism,* actively cultivates selfishness, lack of empathy, and the predatory, primitive instincts of mankind. Long before any socialist state existed, free market capitalism conducted a series of "man made famines" in which millions were needlessly starved. In India, Ireland, Iran, the Arab world, Africa and Asia, the British empire snuffed out the lives of millions of people deemed to be racially inferior. At gunpoint, China was forced to allow British imports to destroy their domestic industries in two "Opium Wars." Under the domination of British bankers, China experienced routine famines and malnutrition related deaths. British settlers in Africa exterminated entire villages with the earliest machine guns. The brutality and inhumanity of the British empire, conducted in the name of "free trade" and "survival of the fittest" has been conveniently forgotten in light of the 20th century. Historians ignore the massive body count of capitalism because it does not fit a political narrative about "anti-totalitarianism."

Nazism is largely an expression of this British capitalism and its supremacist philosophy that views the majority of humanity as "useless eaters." Nazism is not the logical conclusion of German culture or civilization. Until the rise of the Nazi state, Germany was the global stronghold not only of Marxism, but also of art, science, music, and cinema. It was Germany that brought us the music of Bach, Beethoven, and Mozart. The cinema of the Weimar Republic, films such as *Metropolis* and *The Cabinet of Dr. Caligari* are still widely viewed today and viewed as cutting edge in artistic style, rivaling the achievements of Sergei Eisenstein and Soviet Cinema during the same era.

In the 1920s, Berlin was one of the few places on earth where tolerance for sexual minorities was being openly preached. The majority of Germans did not favor the Nazi party. The British imperialists selected the Nazis to rule over Germany as part of the geopolitical game they were playing in the hopes of destroying the Soviet Union. Only after the Reichstag fire and the rounding up of Communist members of parliament were the Nazis able to secure control of the legislature. Never did the German population elect a Nazi majority to the parliament.

The German Communist Party had been the largest Communist Party in the world outside of the USSR. The Social Democratic Party was equally large. Even after the Nazis took power, underground Communist resistance persisted right up until the red army took Berlin. Ernst Thallman was a hero to millions as he sat in the fascist prison, refusing to abandon his principles even under torture.

Today, the British and the Americans are trying to twist the arms of the German people, and force them to cooperate in their efforts to weaken Russia's natural gas pipeline, Nordstream 2. The Germans are expected to pay the excessive costs of importing natural gas from far off countries, rather than purchase it from their Russian neighbors. Much like the propping up of Nazism in order to defeat the German working class movement, the campaign against Nordstream 2 is yet another crime of Wall Street and London in their relentless efforts for greater profits and world domination.

Donald Trump, in his obsession with military strength and his hatred for the most vulnerable in US society, and Kamala Harris, with her gleeful obsession with punishment and revenge, both incarnate different versions of the same distorted thinking. It should not be surprising that admirers of Ayn Rand can be found all across the US political spectrum. Republican Paul Ryan and Democrat Stacey Abrams have both described the demented text *Atlas Shrugged* as their favorite book. This philosophy that scoffs at "love your neighbor as yourself" and celebrates cruelty and lack of empathy is capitalism and liberalism taken to their logical conclusion.

"Single-Minded Son of the Working Class"
We are forced once again to revisit Sigmund Freud and his attempt to interpret the sentiments in religion which others find satisfying. Freud writes of this oceanic feeling he cannot understand that: "A feeling can only be a source of energy if it is itself the expression of a strong need. The derivation of religious needs from the infant's helplessness and the longing for the father aroused by it seems to me to be incontrovertible, especially since the feeling is not simply prolonged from childhood days, but is permanently sustained by fear of the superior power of fate. I cannot think of any need of childhood as strong as the need for a father's protection. Thus the part played by the oceanic feeling, which might seek something like the restoration of limitless narcissism, is ousted from a place in the foreground."

Within human beings, especially in times of hardship and instability, there is a strong desire, not for revenge and chaos or for brutality and cruelty, but rather for a force of strength and power that will protect them and ensure justice. Not only in religion, but in the history of populism in the United States, one can see these desires being fulfilled. The greatest populist leaders in US history have been those who pandered to this desire for strong, effective, compassionate leadership to protect the downtrodden.

When the country was gripped by divisions and economic strife created by the primitive, barbaric practice of chattel slavery, the first mass expression of opposition came in the form of a religious movement called The Second Great Awakening. Reverend Charles G. Finney and others convened Tent Revival meetings and great religious gatherings to denounce slavery, calling for the country to repent from the sinful practice. In the aftermath of this outpouring of religious opposition to slavery, political opposition to it soon emerged on the national stage with the rise of Abraham Lincoln.

Lincoln was a rural lawyer from the wild, newly settled territory of Illinois. He was six feet tall and had a booming voice. He condemned the rich and powerful with statements such as: "These capitalists generally act harmoniously and in concert to fleece the people; and now that they have got into a quarrel with themselves, we are called upon to appropriate the people's money to settle the quarrel." And "It is the eternal struggle between these two principles — right and wrong — throughout the world. They are the two principles that have stood face to face from the beginning of time; and will ever continue to struggle. The one is the common right of humanity, and the other the divine right of kings. It is the same principle in whatever shape it develops itself. It is the same spirit that says, "You toil and work and earn bread, and I'll eat it." No matter in what shape it comes, whether from the mouth of a king who seeks to bestride the people of his own nation and live by the fruit of their labor, or from one race of men as an apology for enslaving another race, it is the same tyrannical principle."

Songs hailed this anti-slavery rabble rouser, saying "Old Abe Lincoln Came Up From the Wilderness." Another anthem widely sung by Lincoln supporters ended with the lines:

Success to the old fashioned doctrine that men are created all free!
Down with the power of the despot, wherever his stronghold may be!

Lincoln was not Trump, a selfish bully displaying crass rudeness and indifference to others. Lincoln was not Kamala Harris, seeking to unleash a torrent of destruction in vengeance for his own perceived victimhood. Lincoln was portrayed as a strong, powerful father figure, ready to beat back the forces of injustice and poverty and defend the helpless.

Karl Marx spoke of him in similar tones, writing in 1864: "The workingmen of Europe feel sure that, as the American War of Independence initiated a new era of ascendancy for the middle class, so the American Antislavery War will do for the working classes. They consider it an earnest of the epoch to come that it fell to the lot of Abraham Lincoln, the single-minded son of the working class, to lead his country through the matchless struggle for the rescue of an enchained race and the reconstruction of a social world."

During the 1930s depression, Huey Long ascended into the political leadership of Louisiana, first as Governor and then as a US Senator. Long built an organization across the United States called the "Share Our Wealth Movement." Long taxed the oil refining of the Rockefellers in Louisiana to bring a large amount of money into the state treasury. He used this money to build hospitals, fund literacy programs, construct bridges, and provide a large number of services for the people of Louisiana. The Black community in particular gained due to Huey Long's efforts. Huey Newton, the founder of the Black Panther Party, was named by his parents in honor of Huey Long. Huey Newton's autobiography *Revolutionary Suicide* describes how Long enabled Black women to become nurses and took other measures to help the Black community, despite the atmosphere of Jim Crow racism.

Long, like Lincoln, presented a personality of strength and compassion. Hailing his achievements for the people of Louisiana, he proclaimed: "We have opened up night schools to educate the adult illiterates. We have paved the highways. We have built free bridges. We have taken the insane out of the jail cells and placed them in modern institutions. We have eliminated barbarism. We have shut down the lottery. We have closed up the gambling dice. We have abolished the vice areas. Now, the corporate element of this state, and the cheap stooges who ransacked this state for their allies, are being told what they can do and what they can't do, what they will pay, and what they won't keep

Huey Long was the Governor of Louisiana during the 1930s. He enacted many progressive policies, building infrastructure and creating an organization called the "Share Our Wealth Movement."

from paying, for the welfare of Louisiana. We expect to have this state ruled by the people, not by the lords and interests of high finance."

Explaining his vision for rescuing the country with the Share Our Wealth movement, he said: "Now, if you have on that table the food and the clothing and the products that it takes for 125 million people to live on, any man with a thimble-full of sense ought to know that if you take 85 percent off of that table and give it to one man, that you are bound to have 2/3 of the people starving because they haven't got enough to eat. How many men ever went to a barbecue and would let one man take off the table what's intended for 9/10ths of the people to eat? The only way you'll ever be able to feed the balance of the people is to make that man come back and bring back some of that grub he ain't got no business with....Now, how you going to feed the balance of the people? What's Morgan and Baruch and Rockefeller and Mellon going to do with all of that grub. They can't eat it. They can't wear the clothes. They can't live in the houses. Give 'em a yacht! Give 'em a palace! Send them to Reno and get them a new wife when they want it, if that's what they want. But when they've got everything on the God's loving earth that they can eat and they can wear and they can live in, and all that their children can live in and wear and eat, and all their children's children can use, then we got to call Mr. Morgan and Mr. Mellon and Mr. Rockefeller back and say, "Come back here. Put that stuff back on this table here that you took away from here -- that you don't need. Leave something else for the American people to consume. And that's the program. We're not going to destroy the Gulf Refining company. We're not going to destroy the Standard Oil company. But we're going to say that the limit of any one man's stock ownership in the Standard Oil company is from 3 to 5 million dollars for that individual, and that the balance of the people in America own the balance of what the Standard Oil company's worth. We're going to say then that every family in this country is entitled to the Florida and the Texas and the Louisiana Homestead rights, up to 5,000 dollars or 1/3 the average. A home! And the comforts of a home! Including an automobile! And a radio! The things that it takes in that house to live on…."

Roosevelt and the Popular Front

As Roosevelt faced opposition in 1936 and moved toward enacting progressive reforms such as the Works Progress Administration and eventually Social Security, he became more and more of a populist himself. The press told of a textile worker in South Carolina shaking Roosevelt's hand and proclaiming he was "the first man in the White House to know my boss is a son-of-a-bitch."

Roosevelt delivered his 1936 speech in Madison Square Garden as he faced widespread opposition from the National Association of Manufacturers and the possible threat of a military coup by fascist sympathizers. These sympathizers had already attempted to do so with the "Business Plot." Roosevelt lambasted his predecessors proclaiming: "For twelve years this Nation was afflicted with hear-nothing, see-nothing, do-nothing Government. The Nation looked to Government but the Government looked away. Nine mocking years with the golden calf and three long years of the scourge! Nine crazy years at the ticker and three long years in the breadlines! Nine mad years of mirage and three long years of despair! Powerful influences strive today to restore that kind of government with its doctrine that that Government is best which is most indifferent."

In 1936 and 1937, Roosevelt gave his support to the Sit-Down Strike Wave in which workers occupied their factories to demand union representation and better conditions.

This notion of laissez-faire, free market, and utopian capitalism long promoted by British bankers and predatory factory owners was thoroughly rejected by Roosevelt. He knew his progressive reforms had faced widespread opposition from the ruling class: "We had to struggle with the old enemies of peace—business and financial monopoly, speculation, reckless banking, class antagonism, sectionalism, war profiteering. They had begun to consider the Government of the United States as a mere appendage to their own affairs. We know now that Government by organized money is just as dangerous as Government by organized mob. Never before in all our history have these forces been so united against one candidate as they stand today. They are unanimous in their hate for me—and I welcome their hatred."

Earl Browder was the Communist Party presidential candidate in 1936, but he made very clear that his campaign was a struggle to defeat the Republicans. The question on the table was "Democracy or Fascism" and Roosevelt's populist program of using the state to provide employment and build infrastructure while mobilizing organized labor was democracy. The plan of the factory owners for resolving the crisis with mass political repression, demonization of the Soviet Union, military spending, and concentration camp labor had to be defeated at all costs.

Communist leaders like William Z. Foster understood that a Popular Front against fascism needed to be formed. The Communist Party stood arm in arm with Roosevelt, a populist, against the Harrises and Trumps of the day and their agenda of low wages, prisons, hostility toward Russia and China, and plans to deal with "overpopulation" by exterminating "useless eaters."

Following the 1936 election, Roosevelt defended the right of workers across the country to occupy their factories in the sit down strike wave of 1936 and 1937. During the episode known as Labor's Gettysburg in Flint, Michigan, Roosevelt sent the military to defend the strikers from the local police and strike breaking militias.

The mass anti-communist hysteria of McCarthyism that set in following the Second World War and Roosevelt's death was necessary because a huge coalition had been built. Roosevelt, the Communist Party, the Congress of Industrial Organizations, the Civil Rights Congress, American Youth for Democracy, and many other progressive, anti-fascist and democratic networks existed, fighting for America's working families and calling for brotherhood and friendship with the people of the world.

The specter of populism, genuine left-wing populism, not Trump's demagogy, now hangs over the United States. It is only a matter of time before movements fighting for the mobilization of state power to protect the suffering millions become bolder and stronger. Such a movement will not come from within the confused, distorted synthetic left any more than it will come from the racism and cruelty of the right. Such a movement can only flourish by going to the masses and addressing their real needs.

A Crisis At Home and Abroad

Who are the geopolitical rivals of the United States? Who are these "authoritarian regimes" US leaders impose sanctions on and condemn with such venomous contempt?

In Latin America, they are the Bolivarians. They are socialists influenced by Marxism, Christianity, Indigenous traditions, and the legacy of anti-colonialism in South and Central America. In Venezuela, Bolivia, Nicaragua, and elsewhere they have instituted public control over natural resources, built roads, wiped out illiteracy, and enabled millions to rise up from poverty.

In China, it is a government that took what was once the "sick man of Asia" and made it into a superpower. The Chinese Communist Party has lifted more than 800 million people from poverty. It has sent spacecraft to the far side of the moon, and has built Huawei, the largest telecommunication manufacturer in the world. With China's mass investment in Fusion energy research, it threatens to render fossil fuels, an essential aspect of Wall Street and London's domination of the global market, to be obsolete.

What Mao Zedong started with a peasant army in the mountains has shaken the world. The Chinese Communist Party's vision of reinventing the global economy on the basis of win-win cooperation points toward a world without war and poverty, and inspires people across the globe. The real achievements of the Asian Infrastructure Investment Bank in terms of building schools, hospitals, and power plants in the developing world point to the promise being more than hollow words.

The current leadership of Russia rescued the country from the disastrous results of the fall of the Soviet Union. This was done by placing oil and natural gas under public control, and centralizing the economy around the state controlled firms, not the anarchy of production. Russia continues to preside over poverty alleviation in the far east and an explosion of the agricultural sector. Russia is cooperating with many African countries to help them expand their economies and continue on a road of poverty alleviation.

The Eurasian Economic Union, the Belt and Road Initiative, and the Bolivarian Alternative for Latin America all stand as contrary examples to the International Monetary Fund, the World Bank and the World Trade Organization. The Bretton Woods Institutions are committed to

The Chinese Communist Party, founded in 1921 with less than 60 members, has led the total economic transformation of the country. Hundreds of Millions of people have been lifted from poverty.

policies of deregulation and demolishing the economies of developing countries. While symbolic self-criticisms about being "too neoliberal" echo from the halls of western global financial centers, these words are hollow bombast. These institutions, like almost all economic discourse in western countries, is predicated on "greed is good" Adam Smith thinking. It is a belief that free trade and control of the global trade routes by western financiers can somehow produce the ideal outcome from humanity.

However, the built-in problem of the capitalist mode of production described by Karl Marx long ago has not gone away. The capitalist is constantly driving to produce more and more goods for as little cost as possible. The capitalist reduces the amount of labor involved in production, replacing it with machines, and creating a falling rate of profit. Machines do not create surplus value, only human labor does.

Machines replace workers on the assembly lines, increasing unemployment. The remaining workers jobs become "de-skilled" by technology, and wages drop as a result. Soon the market is glutted with products that cannot be sold. As the capitalist works to increase profits, the worker is driven to produce harder and harder, but his ability to consume what he produces is constantly reduced.

Soon the market is glutted with products that cannot be sold, the stock market crashes; an unnatural crisis that only takes place in the capitalist mode of production exists. Plenty creates poverty. Abundance leads to want. People become homeless because there are too many houses. People become hungry because there is too much food.

Production organized for profit cannot escape this natural problem. The huge technological leaps brought about by the computer revolution have only exacerbated this problem. The only way out is for the banks, factories, and industries to be organized by state central planners, and forced to work in the interests of society. Production for profit cannot continue.

As millions are unemployed, hungry, and losing their homes amid the economic fallout of the pandemic, the words of Roosevelt about "hear-nothing, see-nothing, do-nothing Government" should be ringing in our ears. As millions suffer, even Bernie Sanders' minimal program of social democratic reforms couldn't be tolerated by the oligarchy of oil bankers, prison profiteers, weapons manufacturers, and silicon valley fascists who run the United States of America. Millions are now outcast and starving, watching their country crumble with unpaved roads, improperly purified water, and a failing systems of education and healthcare.

Trump could not liquidate this crisis. Kamala Harris will be equally impotent.

As racist statues are torn down by liberal protesters, and Trump's demagogy leads toward even greater instability, the longing on the part of much of the population isn't for violence and vengeance. There is a strong desire for that oceanic feeling of one-ness, solidarity, and human life, the glue that holds civilizations together and enables whole societies to rise up from the ashes.

There is a longing for leadership that is not cynical and bigoted or vengeful and destructive. There is a longing for a real government of action that can fight for those who are suffering, bring a divided country together, smash the rule of big bankers and profiteers, and completely reinvent the country.

The ruling elite knows that the specter of populism, the specter of 21st Century Socialism, is hanging over their heads. It is not the specter of a foreign conspiracy or a demagogic politician, but the recognition that the people of the country will soon be rising in the millions to demand a society that puts their needs first.

Printed in Great Britain
by Amazon